Snakes

David Gower,

Katherine Garrett

and Peter Stafford

FIREFLY BOOKS

A FIREFLY BOOK

Published by Firefly Books Ltd. 2012

First printing

Publisher Cataloging-in-Publication Data (U.S.)

Stafford, Peter
    Snakes / Peter Stafford ; with Katherine Garrett and David Gower.
[144] p. : col. photos. ; cm.
Includes bibliographical references and index.
Summary: The biology and natural history of this ecologically important group of animals, with information on habitat, conservation status, and unusual behavior.
ISBN-13: 978-1-55407-802-8 (pbk.)
1. Snakes. I. Gower, David. II. Title.
597.96 dc22   QL666.O6S75   2012

Library and Archives Canada Cataloguing in Publication

Stafford, Peter J.
    Snakes / Peter Stafford with Katherine Garrett and David Gower.
Includes bibliographical references and index.
ISBN 978-1-55407-802-8
    1. Snakes. I. Gower, David J., 1969- II. Title.
QL666.O6S73 2012   597.96   C2011-906141-4

Published in the United States by
Firefly Books (U.S.) Inc.
P.O. Box 1338, Ellicott Station
Buffalo, New York 14205

Published in Canada by
Firefly Books Ltd.
66 Leek Crescent
Richmond Hill, Ontario L4B 1H1

Printed in China by C&C Offset

Developed by:
The Natural History Museum
Cromwell Road, London SW7 5BD

Designed by Mercer Design, London
Reproduction by Saxon Digital Services

Front and back cover: © Michael D. Kern/naturepl.com

Contents

Preface

FEW ANIMALS EVOKE SUCH STRONG EMOTIONS in humans as snakes – they are loathed, feared, admired, or even worshipped the world over. There can be hardly anyone without at least some perception of these distinctive and fascinating animals. But what exactly is it that inspires these feelings? For many it is undoubtedly because some snakes have deadly bites, but for most of us it is probably because they are difficult to relate to. How can an animal so long and thin move so gracefully without limbs, or swallow a meal several times larger than its head, and what is it that enables some snakes to survive without eating for months?

The first objective of this book is to answer some of these questions. Its other main purpose is to explore each of the main groups of snakes and convey some impression of the remarkable extent to which these animals have diversified. Snakes inhabit almost every part of the globe where temperatures remain conducive to life for at least part of the year, including the open sea, and they have become specialized for living in a wide range of different environments. Some are adapted for life in water and never venture onto dry land, while others are found only in the treetops of rainforests, or spend much of their lives burrowing underground in dry, sandy deserts or moist tropical soils. Only in the coldest regions and on some islands (notably Ireland and New Zealand) are there none at all. Equally varied and complex are the ways in which individual species live, and by focusing on aspects of their natural history we hope that this book will encourage the growing appreciation of snakes as an important group of animals that should be valued and admired rather than feared and hated.

The history of this book deserves explanation because it includes a fine pedigree of books written by staff of the Natural History Museum, London. The origin lies with the 1963 book *Snakes* written by Hampton W Parker CBE (1897–1968), an expert herpetologist who was Keeper (head of the department) of Zoology between 1947 and 1957. This 1963 book was reincarnated by Parker in a modified version as *Natural History of Snakes* in 1965, and that version was expanded and revised by Alice G C Grandison in 1977 when it was published as *Snakes – A Natural History*. Grandison considered this 1977 version to be a second edition of Parker's 1965 book. Grandison (b.1927) was head of the Natural History Museum's herpetology section, where she worked between 1951 and 1984. The 1977 version (and its antecedents) was clearly an influence on Peter J Stafford's 2000 book *Snakes*. Stafford (1961–2009) was employed by the museum as a botanist, but moonlighted as a herpetologist and was widely known outside the museum for his studies of amphibians and reptiles. The 2000 book was the first to use a very extensive set of photographs, but it also included several of the figures that Brian C Groombridge had drawn for the 1977 version, and these figures are also included in this new version. All four previous versions have covered aspects of snake natural history as well as summarizing their taxonomic, ecological and morphological diversity, and we follow that model here. This new version was built directly from Peter Stafford's book and much is owed to it and its predecessors.

ABOUT THE AUTHORS

DAVID J GOWER is an organismal biologist whose research covers such wide-ranging aspects as evolution, taxonomy, biogeography, ecology, reproduction and conservation. His research is firmly rooted in natural history collections, and his taxon expertise lies in caecilian amphibians and Triassic archosaurian reptiles as well as (mostly burrowing and aquatic) snakes. He has published more than 100 articles in scientific journals, and frequently conducts herpetological fieldwork in the moist tropics. He is a researcher and co-leader of the Herpetology Research Group in the Natural History Museum, London, Section Editor for snakes and caecilians for the international journal *Zootaxa*, and Editor in Chief of the Systematics Association.

KATHERINE GARRETT works in the Botany Department of the Natural History Museum, London, composing a biographical database of botanical specimen collectors. Long interested in amphibians and reptiles, she is also a volunteer in the museum's Herpetology Research Group. She has participated in several herpetological field projects, including surveying amphibians in Cameroon, and conducting research on leatherback sea turtles in Costa Rica.

PETER STAFFORD was a pollen biologist in the Botany Department at the Natural History Museum, London, until his untimely death in 2009. He had held a keen interest in amphibians and reptiles, particularly snakes, since a boy, and was involved with studies on the biology of these animals for many years. Among his numerous publications he is credited with having written or co-authored several books on the subject of herpetology, including *The Adder*, a popular book on the natural history of this venomous snake in Britain, and most recently a comprehensive guide to the reptiles found in Belize, Central America. Peter was a member of several herpetological societies and the editor of the *British Herpetological Society Bulletin*.

PART ONE

Structure and lifestyle

APPROXIMATELY 3,300 LIVING SPECIES of snakes have been discovered and formally described and named. They range in size from the burrowing thread snakes that may be as little as 10 cm (4 in) long, to giants such as the larger pythons and boas that grow to 7 m (23 ft) or more. Some specialized tree-living kinds are amazingly long and thin, whereas many of the vipers, boas and pythons are relatively short and heavy-set, and there is a whole range of different combinations in between.

While they vary in size and shape, the features that collectively distinguish snakes as a group are, however, clearly recognizable: the body is greatly lengthened and highly flexible, there are no apparent limbs, and the eyes have no eyelids. They differ further from other reptiles in lacking any sign of a shoulder girdle, forelimbs and a sternum (breastbone), and in the vast majority there are no vestiges either of a pelvis or hindlimbs. Only pythons, boas and a few other forms have remains of hindlimbs, which appear externally as small, horn-like claws at the base of the tail, and some remnant of a pelvis.

OPPOSITE A grass snake, the natricine colubrid *Natrix natrix*, in Tuscany, Italy.

LEFT The ancestors of snakes may have looked superficially like the slow-worm, *Anguis fragilis*, an Old World lizard that, like snakes, has lost its legs and acquired an elongate body.

THE ORIGINS AND FOSSIL RECORD OF SNAKES

Snakes (sometimes considered to form the suborder Serpentes) are members of the order Squamata. Squamates comprise all living reptiles except for crocodiles and alligators (Order Crocodylia), tortoises and turtles (Order Testudines) and the tuatara (Order Sphenodontia). Thus, squamates include all living snakes and lizards. Evolutionary relationships within Squamata have been a matter of ongoing debate, but the most recent DNA analyses indicate that snakes' closest living relatives are anguimorphs (monitor lizards, beaded lizards, knob-scaled lizards, galliwasps, slow worms, glass lizards and alligator lizards) and/or iguanians (iguanas, chameleons, anoles and agamas). Whatever the precise relationships among snakes and other squamates, it is clear that snakes arose from lizard-like ancestors.

The many divergent features of snakes, including their elongate and limbless body form and unusual eyes, have resulted in two main competing explanations for snake origins. The dominant hypothesis is that snakes underwent a burrowing phase in their immediate ancestry or early history. The supporting evidence lies in the observation that several lineages of lizards (e.g. slow worms, dibamids, amphisbaenians, pygopod geckos) have become elongate and have lost or substantially reduced their limbs, and these all burrow in sand or soil. Some of the peculiarities of snake eyes are the result of evolutionary loss of some ancestral features, and this is also known to have occurred to varying degrees in other burrowing vertebrates. The main competing hypothesis is that snakes passed through a profoundly aquatic (and marine) phase in their immediate ancestry. Although some scientists have claimed that snake eyes are similar in several features to those of other aquatic vertebrates, the main supporting evidence for the marine hypothesis comes from several snake fossils that retain hindlimbs and that were fossilized in marine sediments deposited in the Cretaceous period (145 to 65 million years ago). Proponents of this marine hypothesis argue that elongation of the body and

BELOW Fossil of the extinct marine snake *Eupodophis descouensi* preserved in Cretaceous rocks from Lebanon, nearly 100 million years old. The left image shows the whole specimen peserved in a slab of rock. The right image shows a close-up of part of the vertebral column and a small but well-formed right hindlimb, with part of the ankle and the foot missing.

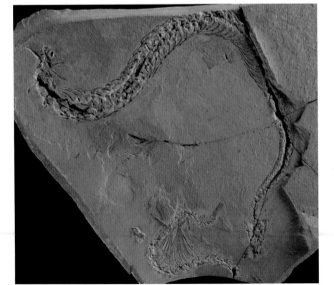

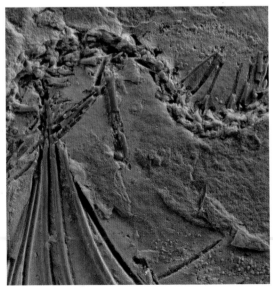

reduction of limbs arose as an adaptation to swimming in water rather than burrowing on land. The marine hypothesis has been weakened by evidence that the Cretaceous limbed snakes are not close to the immediate ancestry of living snakes, but are instead probably embedded more deeply within the evolutionary tree of living snakes, so that their limbs might have partly re-evolved from small stubs such as are retained in, for example, living pythons.

Although the marine Cretaceous snakes are known from some spectacular and complete fossil specimens, the fossil record of snakes generally is very patchy and largely fragmentary. Many snake fossils consist of no more than isolated vertebrae. Interpreting these fossils can be difficult because even vertebral variation within and among individuals and species of living snakes is not well known in detail. It is particularly tricky to identify the earliest member of any major group of organisms based on fragmentary fossils, and this is true also for snakes. Geologically the oldest snake reported thus far is from Cretaceous rocks in North America dating to about 98.5 million years ago. An older fossil find from Spain (between 132 and 124 million years old) was claimed previously to be a snake, but its vertebral anatomy is not distinct enough from that of lizards to be sure. Other important fossils that date a minimum age for some groups of snakes include viper and elapid fangs from German deposits of between 23 and 20 million years old, scolecophidian remains from about 65 million year old rocks in Texas, and approximately 84 million year old python- or boa-like remains from Argentina. Future fossil discoveries are likely to have a dramatic impact on our understanding of the timing and pattern of the evolutionary diversification of snakes.

ABOVE A fossil vertebra of the extinct giant snake *Titanoboa cerrejonensis*, excavated from rocks approximately 60 million years old in Colombia. This species reached lengths of at least 13 m (42½ ft), and the fossil specimen shown here dwarfs a similar vertebra of a 5.2 m (17 ft) long modern day green anaconda, *Eunectes murinus* (also see p.60).

ANATOMY

Over the course of evolution, elongation of the snake's body has necessitated the modification and rearrangement of its internal organs. Most of the main organs themselves are present and not very different from those of humans and other vertebrates, but they have changed so much in shape and position that it can be difficult to recognize them at first glance.

The lungs in particular have undergone considerable modification. Some snakes have two lungs, but in these cases the left is always smaller than the right. In some pythons the left lung can be up to 85% of the length of the right lung, but in the majority of snakes the left lung has been either lost completely or become greatly reduced, as little as 1% of the length of the right in some lamprophiids. In some aquatic snakes, such as the Asian/Australasian file snakes (*Acrochordus*), the right lung is particularly large, extending backwards for nearly the entire length of the body. A possibly additional respiratory area in many snakes is provided by a special modification of the windpipe, known as the tracheal lung.

In most vertebrates, paired organs such as the kidneys and gonads usually lie in the same position on either side of the body, but these have become staggered in the elongate body of snakes. Among other organs affected by the radical change in body shape is the stomach, which has become greatly enlarged and in some snakes accounts for more than one-third of the total length of the body. There is also no urinary bladder; nitrogenous waste is voided not in a solution of urea, as in humans and almost all other mammals, but in a semi-solid state as uric acid, as in lizards and birds. The heart has three chambers, as opposed to four in humans, while the male copulatory organ is a pair of structures, called hemipenes (as also found in lizards), variously and sometimes spectacularly adorned with frills and spines and other ornamentation.

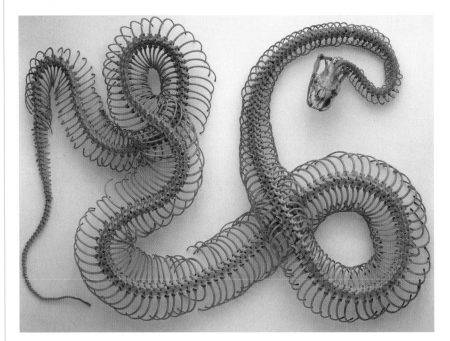

TOP RIGHT A snake's skeleton is comprised mostly of vertebrae and pairs of ribs. There is no sternum, shoulder girdle or forelimbs, although in some, such as this *Python*, vestiges of the pelvis and hindlimbs remain.

RIGHT The everted paired hemipenes of a male snake. Biologists often use the details of size, shape and ornamentation of these structures to help distinguish different species.

THE ANATOMY OF A MALE SNAKE

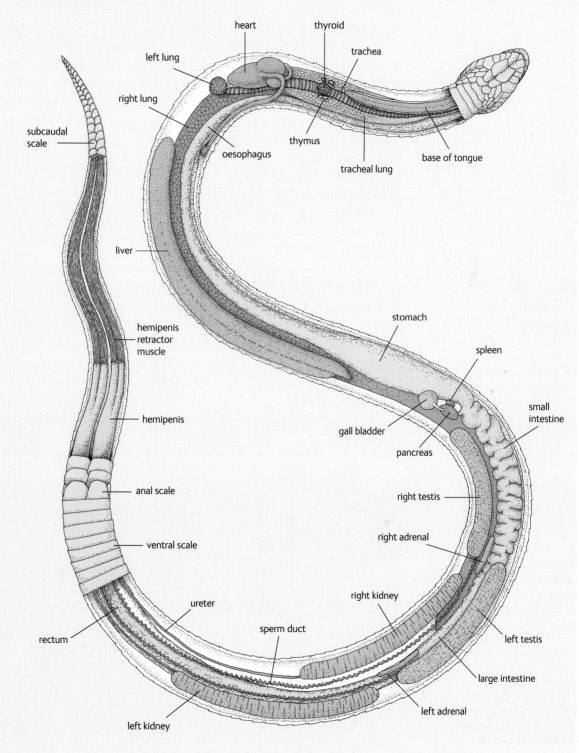

SKULL AND TEETH

The most distinctive feature of the skull in the majority of snakes is its remarkably flexible construction. With some exceptions (e.g. pipe snakes), most of a snake's skull bones are movably connected to each other and attached only loosely to the braincase, so that much of the head is capable of being stretched and distorted in many directions. The two halves of the lower jaw are not fused at the front into a solid 'chin', but are often separated by elastic ligaments that allow them to be forced apart when the snake is swallowing large prey. The suppleness of the lower jaw is further enhanced by a joint in the middle of each of its two halves that enables the jaws to be flexed outwards. The lower jaws connect to the skull via the quadrate bones. In many snakes the quadrates are elongate and their lower ends can swivel outwards, allowing the rear ends of the lower jaws to be forced apart and large prey to pass into the throat.

The teeth of snakes are thorn-shaped and recurved and some species may have a great many of them. As well as those lining each of the upper and lower jaws, there are normally two further rows on the roof of the mouth (the palatine and pterygoid bones). Snake teeth are replaced alternately and repeatedly throughout life. Stiletto snakes, some colubrids, elapids and vipers have one or more pairs of enlarged teeth that are specially modified for injecting venom, and the teeth of certain other species are suited for eating particular kinds of prey. Those of the Central American neck-banded snake (the scaphiodontophiine colubrid *Scaphiodontophis annulatus*), for example, are slightly flattened at their tips for grasping the smooth, hard-scaled bodies of skinks on which it largely feeds. The teeth of this snake are also hinged on flexible ligaments that enable them to be locked into a backward-pointing position when prey is being swallowed, thus preventing it from struggling free.

BELOW Skull of a python, *Python sebae*. Annotations refer to bones mentioned in this book. Note in particular the coronoid bone, a primitive feature of the lower jaw that has been lost in many snakes.

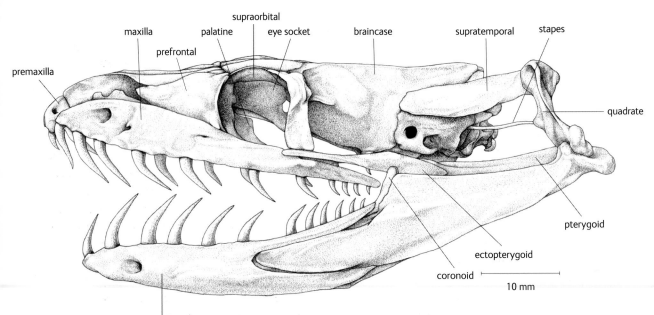

TYPES OF DENTITION IN SNAKES

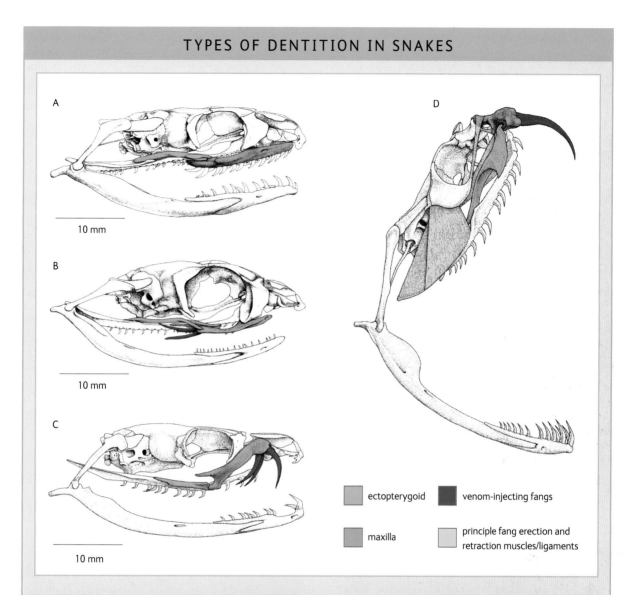

A

10 mm

B

10 mm

C

10 mm

D

ectopterygoid   venom-injecting fangs

maxilla   principle fang erection and retraction muscles/ligaments

Features shaded represent the main components of the biting mechanism; note in particular the relative sizes of the maxillary bone.

A No enlarged fangs (aglyphous). Includes thread/blind snakes, pipe snakes, sunbeam snakes, boas, pythons and many non-venomous colubroids.

B Enlarged, rear-mounted fangs usually preceded on the maxilla by several smaller, unmodified teeth (opisthoglyphous). Includes aparallactine lamprophiids and many venomous colubroids.

C Enlarged, forward-mounted fangs that are non-erectile (proteroglyphous). Includes cobras, mambas, coral snakes and all other elapids.

D Greatly reduced maxilla bone with enlarged, forward-mounted fangs that are erectile and capable of being pivoted independently (solenoglyphous); when not in use the fangs fold back along the upper jaw. Includes stiletto snakes (atractaspidine lamprophiids) and all vipers, though in these two groups the nature of the articulation between the maxilla and the prefrontal is different. All fangs are on the upper jaws, and these enlarged teeth are also tubular or grooved to facilitate the delivery of venom into prey.

The presence and position of different types of fangs used to be of prime importance in previous classifications of the major lineages of snakes. It is now known that evolutionary changes among the main different types of dentition have occurred several times. Thus, even closely related snakes might not necessarily share the same types of dentition, so teeth are not always a reliable guide to evolutionary relationships. Recently, detailed modern studies of developmental biology have demonstrated that in all snakes with fangs these enlarged teeth develop first at the rear of the upper jaw, and that in front-fanged snakes (e.g. vipers, elapids) they migrate forwards during development. Thus, front fangs of different snake lineages probably have a common developmental origin, but the anterior migration has evolved independently in different groups.

Developmental studies have also shown that tubular venom-delivering fangs of elapids and vipers grow their tubes not by a progressive infolding of the long edges of the teeth, but by adding more tooth material around the base of an incipient tube that is present when the teeth first form. Snakes with tubular fangs have muscles associated with their venom glands that squeeze the venom out at the high pressure needed to move it forcibly through the narrow bore of the needle-like teeth and into the flesh of prey. It has been argued that tubular fangs are ancestral for colubroid snakes (and were subsequently simplified or lost in several lineages) rather than evolving independently at least three times – in elapids, vipers and atractaspidine lamprophiids.

SKIN, SCALES AND MOULTING

As in other reptiles, the entire surface of the body of almost all snakes is covered with scales (for an exception see p.76). On the head these may be large (sometimes termed 'shields') and arranged in a symmetrical pattern, or small and irregular. Those on the upper surface and sides of the body (dorsals) are usually small and regular, sometimes with a horizontal ridge across the centre (keeled), while the scales on the belly (ventrals) are typically large and broad and extend crosswise in a single row between the head and base of the tail. In some snakes the scales beneath the tail (subcaudals) are also arranged in a single row, while in others they are paired. In some snakes the scales of the snout and chin are covered with microscopic sensory tubercles that appear to be associated with reproduction, and similar tubercles occur near the base of the tail in certain New World coral snakes.

The outermost layer of a snake's skin consists of a continuous sheet of keratin, a rather inflexible material also found in your fingernails and hair. Derived from dead cells, this layer must be shed every so often to allow for growth and repair. The frequency with which this shedding, or sloughing, occurs depends primarily on the rate of growth, and young healthy snakes, which grow more quickly, slough their skins more often.

In the initial stages of this process, the skin loses its usual fresh appearance and turns milky-white, due to the secretion of a lubricant beneath the redundant upper layer: this is especially pronounced over the eyes. It persists for several days and may take up to three weeks before it finally clears, during which time the snake is often

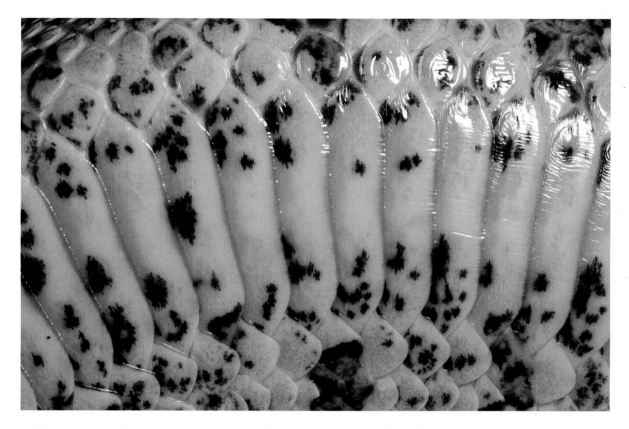

unable to see properly and will usually remain hidden away. Many snakes also refuse to feed during this period, and if disturbed may be irascible.

A few days after fully regaining its sight, the snake becomes restless and begins to rub its head against the ground, stones, or other rough surfaces until the old skin separates at the tip of the snout and along the jawline, from where it then peels back over the rest of the body as the snake moves around. In the process, the old skin is turned inside out. Aquatic snakes that live in open water, such as sea snakes, cannot always find suitable rough surfaces, but some of these species have ingeniously solved the problem by coiling themselves into knots and rubbing one part of the body against another.

The very fine texture (micro-ornamentation) of the surface of scales is adapted to serve different purposes depending on the ecology of the snake in question. For example, ventral scales of ground-dwelling snakes are often shiny and seem to be smooth, probably partly to reduce friction as they slide their bellies along the substrate, but also because the underside of the snake is rarely seen and so even if it is shiny it will not alert predators or prey to the snake's presence. For the same reason, many snakes have much duller and light-absorbing/scattering (rather than reflecting) dorsal scales. Many soil-dwelling burrowing (fossorial) snakes have exceptionally iridescent scales. This iridescence probably serves no immediate function, but it appears to be an accidental consequence of evolving scales that are covered in very regularly spaced, microscopic ridges – features that serve to repel moisture and dirt.

ABOVE Individual scales of a snake's body are separated by interconnecting skin that is generally concealed beneath. This allows for the considerable flexibility needed for movement or consuming large meals. The broad scales on this ground boa from Madagascar, *Acrantophis dumerili*, are the 'ventrals' along the midline of the belly.

EXPLOITATION OF SNAKES

The largest threat to snake populations around the world is undoubtedly from habitat loss, but their exploitation as a resource for human consumption poses a great threat to some of the world's species. Although it is very difficult to compile accurate figures for the number of snakes traded around the world, in Southeast Asia alone between 1998 and 2007 at least 1.8 million cobras and 1.2 million pythons were traded.

It has been estimated that in China between 7 and 9 million kilograms of snakes are traded each year. China is one of the major players in the use of snakes for human consumption (including as medicine) and hundreds of snake products can be found in Chinese markets. The habit of eating snakes has spread across the country in recent years and, although China was primarily an exporter of snake products, it is increasingly becoming a major importer. Although nobody can say yet for sure, this may be because of the depletion of China's indigenous snake populations. Species of the colubrid genus *Elaphe* (rat snakes) are among the most important traded in this country. The world's single largest snake harvest occurs in the lake of Tonle Sap in Cambodia, where 7 million snakes, mostly homalopsids, are caught each year for meat, skin and crocodile food (see p.92).

Live snakes are also collected and sold throughout the world, primarily for the pet trade, with a relatively small number also going to zoos and research institutions. The pet trade is substantial in Europe and North America as well as Asia. Figures from CITES, the Convention on International Trade in Endangered Species of Wild Flora and Fauna (the body that regulates trade in wildlife), show that nearly 300,000 live snakes were traded in 1992, with the most important species being the oriental rat snake (the colubrid *Ptyas mucosa*), followed by the ball python, *Python regius*, and the Indian cobra, *Naja naja*.

Although the numbers of individuals captured for the pet trade industry are considerable, they do not come anywhere near those taken for their skins. Snake skin is admired by some people the world over for its attractive colours and patterns and has been highly prized by the leather industry ever since large-scale commercial harvesting of these animals began in the early 1900s. Many species are exploited for this purpose, but perhaps none more heavily than the reticulated python, *Broghammerus reticulatus*, of which thousands are exported each year. Indonesia is by far the largest exporter of this species with the CITES quota for this country alone standing at 162,000 individuals for 2010. Of these, 3% are traded live while the remainder were exported either as raw skins or processed products (mainly shoes, boots and handbags). The real number of reticulated pythons harvested in Southeast Asia per year is thought to be close to 500,000.

The sheer volume of snakes known to have been harvested for their skins globally during particular years is alarming. Based on CITES data, conservationists calculated that in 1985, for example, the leather industry used 1,449,475 m of snake skin – that is, almost 1,450 km (885 miles)! Furthermore, this is an extremely conservative estimate because it includes only anacondas and large pythons, and not the many other, smaller snake species exploited for this purpose, such as various boas, Asian rat snakes, short-tailed pythons, Asian/Australasian file snakes, mud snakes (see p.92), cobras and sea snakes.

Wild snakes are also collected by scientists and preserved as museum specimens that are used in a diversity of biological research projects. Scientific collecting is generally tightly controlled and involves relatively small numbers. Non-commercial and responsible scientific collecting is not known to have threatened the conservation status of any snake species, and is often essential in generating the taxonomic, distributional and ecological data that underpins effective conservation biology.

SENSES

Snakes have an acute sense of chemoreception (odour detection). Odorants are detected using two independent systems, the 'nose' (olfactory system) and the vomeronasal (or Jacobson's) organ in the roof of the mouth. The nose smells odorants drawn in through the nostrils, while the vomeronasal organ senses odorants that are picked up physically by the tongue as it flicks in and out of the mouth. Although the two systems are somewhat disconnected and use different signalling pathways, it seems that sensing by olfaction is important for increasing the rate of tongue flicking. So acute is the snake's sense of chemoreception that it can detect even the faintest scent trails left by prey – or another snake. The specialist ant- and termite-hunting scolecophidian snakes, for example, can accurately follow an ant trail even a week after the trail has been made.

ABOVE As well as using their nose, snakes detect odour by using their tongue to transfer odorants to the vomeronasal (Jacobson's) organ in the roof of the mouth. The tongue may also have a tactile function.

SIGHT

In most snakes vision is quite well developed, but by human standards many are probably rather short-sighted. Snakes' eyes are different from those of other animals. In humans and most other vertebrates, for example, focusing is achieved with special muscles that change the shape of the lens, whereas in most snakes there are no such muscles and images are focused instead by the lens moving physically towards or away from the retina. Snake retinas are also interesting in that, as a group, they have a greater diversity of photoreceptor cell types than other vertebrates, though the functional and evolutionary significance of this is not understood. Biologists still know very little about how snakes see, but it seems that for many species their eyes will be used to detect movement rather than forming very detailed images: snakes hunting by sight will often fail to recognize a potential meal unless it begins to move, even if it is only a few centimetres away.

LEFT Snakes do not have eyelids. Instead the eyes are covered by a transparent protective cap (the brille), as in this Neotropical bird snake, the colubrine colubrid *Pseustes poecilonotus*.

HEARING

Snakes have neither an external ear nor an eardrum, although the sense of hearing in many species appears to be otherwise fairly well developed. It is best suited to detecting ground vibrations, picked up by the bones of the lower jaw and transmitted to the inner ear via a delicate, bony rod (the stapes). Recent research suggests that the ear of many snakes may be more sensitive to airborne sound than has previously been assumed, and some herpetologists think the lung may also act as a resonator.

OTHER SENSES

Rattlesnakes and other pit vipers, together with some (perhaps all) pythons and boas, are unique among vertebrates in having a sense organ that detects infrared radiation. These organs in pit vipers are in a special pit on the side of the face, while in pythons and boas they are within, between or behind scales along the lips. The thermal information is combined in the brain simultaneously with visual images from the eyes, allowing these snakes to form very rich and detailed 'pictures' of their environment. Vipers are able to detect radiation emitted by 'warm-blooded' prey at distances of up to 1 m (3¼ ft). The pit organs of many pit vipers might even be able to detect very small differences in temperature between 'cold-blooded' animals such as frogs and the environment and thus locate them in the dark.

Just as remarkable, the nocturnal olive sea snake, *Aipysurus laevis*, has light-sensitive organs on its tail that it apparently uses to ensure that the tail is not left exposed when it is hiding among crevices during the day (see p.108).

TEMPERATURE REGULATION

Snakes, and reptiles in general, are ectothermic animals that depend almost entirely on external sources of heat and must regulate their body temperatures by behavioural means. To achieve their optimum 'working' temperature they expose themselves to whatever source of heat may be available, such as direct sunlight or a sun-warmed rock. Should they begin to overheat, they cool down by moving into shade, burrowing underground, or immersing themselves in water. They must keep their body temperature within a range of about 4–38°C (39–100°F); if it should fall or rise only a few degrees either side of these levels, they can die.

At times when prevailing conditions make it impossible for snakes to reach or regulate their body temperatures, they escape by retreating to a state of dormancy (aestivation). During the freezing conditions of winter in northern Europe, for example, adders, *Vipera berus*, hibernate in underground dens for up to eight months of the year, while in some tropical regions that have long, hot, dry seasons, many snakes will secrete themselves in a cool burrow or beneath the bark of a tree and aestivate to avoid the effects of dehydration. Despite their reliance on external heat sources and the often cool feel to their bodies when handled, a snake's body temperature can be as high as our own after only a short time basking in the sun, and it is thus misleading to refer to these animals as 'cold-blooded'.

HOW SNAKES MOVE

ABOVE A horned adder, the viperid *Bitis caudalis*, 'sidewinding' over a desert sand dune in Namibia.

How snakes move is one of their most intriguing features. Part of the answer lies in their large number of vertebrae and ribs, which provide the extra flexibility needed for limbless locomotion. Whereas humans have 43 vertebrae, some species of snakes have over 500. The vertebrae of snakes are among the most elaborate and complex found in any backboned animals, with a whole range of structures for supporting the ligaments and tendons that enable them to move in their characteristic 'slithery' manner.

Most snakes proceed with continuous side to side undulations formed by the natural progression of the body as it follows in line behind the head, where forward movement is achieved by the animal using each of the resulting S-shaped loops to push against irregularities in the ground. If the ground over which the snake is moving is unstable, as with loose, shifting sand, or there are no stones, twigs or other adequate 'footholds' which its body can push against, its ability to move is seriously impaired.

Many of the larger, stouter-bodied snakes, such as pythons, boas and ground-dwelling vipers, can also employ 'rectilinear' locomotion, whereby they move along with the body extended in almost a straight line. It used to be thought that this was achieved by effectively 'walking' on the tips of their ribs, but the ribs stay in position and instead groups of ventral scales are raised, moved forward and then placed back down on the ground and the body is drawn forwards over them. Another form of locomotion used by heavy-bodied snakes and also by many burrowing and climbing forms is the 'concertina crawl', in which the animal advances by reaching ahead and pushing its body against the ground, a branch or some other firm point of anchorage, from where it is then able to pull the rest of its body up behind.

In sandy deserts or other areas where there is no firm ground, several kinds of snakes have developed a modified form of progression known as sidewinding. They throw the body into a succession of S-shaped coils and, instead of the more usual 'slither', take a succession of obliquely oriented 'steps' over the ground, during which the body is in contact with the surface at only two points at any given moment. The best-known exponents of this type of movement are desert-living vipers.

FEEDING AND DIET

All snakes are carnivorous. Under natural conditions they feed more or less exclusively on living prey. A few will occasionally eat carrion (e.g. the diet of some North American cottonmouth vipers, *Agkistrodon piscivorus*, includes fish regurgitated by parent seabirds attending nestlings), but this tends to be the exception rather than the rule. Many of the more slender and agile snakes forage actively for prey, while others, such as boas, pythons and vipers, are mostly ambush-hunters that lunge from a hiding place at passing animals. The predatory strike of a snake is often too fast to follow, and in some species is delivered with such force that much of the body may be thrown forwards. A number of the vipers and several other ambush-hunters have contrastingly coloured tails to lure prey within striking range (see p.79), and the African vine/twig snake (the colubrid *Thelotornis capensis*) is said to use its brilliantly coloured red tongue to attract prey in much the same way.

SWALLOWING PREY

Snakes normally swallow their prey whole, although there are a few instances where they may first discard some body parts. Thread/blind snakes, for example, may break off the heads of termites before swallowing them, and white-bellied mangrove snakes (the homalopsid *Fordonia leucobalia*) will twist the legs off a crab if the animal itself is too large to swallow in one piece.

The size of prey eaten by some snakes is truly amazing. Green anacondas, *Eunectes murinus*, and several species of large python are well known for their

BELOW Spotted python, the Australo-Papuan *Antaresia maculosus*, constricting a rat. Coils thrown around the body of the victim prevent if from inhaling and death is brought about by suffocation.

ability to consume deer, pigs and occasionally even humans, while small African egg-eating snakes (the colubrid *Dasypeltis*), with heads scarcely wider than a fingernail, can swallow a hen's egg (see p.126). Some vipers have been known to ingest meals exceeding 150% of their own body weight. Such incredible feats of swallowing are made possible by the development in many snakes of an enormously distensible and flexible mouth (see p.12). Because they have no sternum (breastbone), the ends of the ribs can also separate widely to allow large prey to pass into the stomach.

Many non-venomous snakes begin swallowing as soon as they have secured a firm grip on their prey, whereas burrowing asps, elapids, vipers and some rear-fanged snakes first produce paralysis or death in their victim with venom. Others, such as the pythons and boas, first immobilize prey by suffocating it within the coils of their bodies.

A snake usually starts swallowing as soon as it has adjusted its victim into a head-first position. It extends the upper and lower jaws on each side of its head forwards in turn over and around the prey so that, after several repetitions of these movements, the prey is slowly manoeuvred backwards into the throat, eased along during the process by a lubricating coat of saliva. Wave-like contractions of the oesophagus then push the animal down into the snake's stomach. The snake may take up to an hour or more to swallow large, bulky prey, so with the mouth and throat often completely filled during this period how does it avoid suffocation? The answer is that it can keep its airway open during swallowing because the end of the windpipe (glottis) is strengthened with rings of cartilage, and a further modification enables the glottis to be extended forwards along the floor of the mouth so that breathing can continue unimpeded.

ABOVE Spotted cat-eyed snake, the dipsadine colubrid *Leptodeira septentrionalis*, swallowing a frog. The ability of many snakes to swallow large prey is made possible by the development of an enormously distensible mouth and elastic skin.

DIFFERENT DIETS

Whereas many snakes eat a wide range of prey, others have highly specialized food preferences. Some feed almost exclusively on lizards, birds or rodents, and there are many that eat nothing but frogs. Among the most unusual dietary specialists are scolecophidian snakes (see p.41), which feed almost exclusively on ants, termites and their pupae, the African egg-eating snakes (see p.126), snail-eaters (see p.76, p.131), Central American scorpion-eaters, and some sea snakes that eat only fish eggs (see p.110). Other kinds of prey exploited by specialist feeders include reptile eggs, earthworms, centipedes, bats, crabs, salamanders and amphisbaenians (burrowing snake-like reptiles), and a surprisingly large number of species have a diet that consists chiefly of other snakes.

Some species, such as the Australian taipan (the elapid *Oxyuranus scutellatus*) and the black mamba (the elapid *Dendroaspis polylepis*) of Africa, live on one or two kinds of prey throughout their entire lives, whereas the food preferences of many others vary according to their age and size, the time of year, or geographical location. Juvenile striped swamp snakes (the natricine colubrid *Regina alleni*) of North America, for example, eat shrimp and dragonfly nymphs, whereas adults feed entirely on crayfish. Water pythons, *Liasis fuscus*, in Australia subsist on floodplain rats during the dry season and change to a diet of water birds and their eggs in the rainy season (see p.55), while Mexican parrot snakes (the colubrine colubrid *Leptophis mexicanus*) eat frogs on mainland Central America and mostly lizards on some of the offshore islands.

A well-known feature of snakes is the ability of some species to survive without food for long periods. Pregnant female anacondas in the wild, for example, do not normally eat for the entire six to eight months of gestation, and black tiger snakes (the elapid *Notechis ater*) on Mount Chappell Island in the Bass Straight off southern Australia may feed for only a few weeks per year when their principal prey, the chicks of muttonbirds, are available. The longest recorded interval during which a snake has survived without food is held jointly by a green anaconda, *Eunectes murinus*, and an African rock python, *Python sebae*, both of which apparently refused food in captivity for three years before eating again! Under normal circumstances, snakes maintain themselves in a continuous state of readiness for feeding, but if food becomes scarce and there are lengthy intervals between meals, the internal organs of some species reduce to a state of temporary suspension (see p.57).

VENOM

According to their principal clinical effects, snake venoms are normally classified as either neurotoxic (attacking nerve tissues and interfering with the transmission of nerve impulses), or haemotoxic (directed towards the blood and circulatory system). Neurotoxic venoms are characteristic mainly of elapid snakes, such as cobras, mambas and coral snakes, bites from which affect the central nervous

system and typically lead to death by muscle paralysis and respiratory failure. The haemotoxic venoms of vipers cause tissue destruction, swelling and blood loss, and death usually results from hypotensive shock as blood pressure drops to a point where the heart can no longer function. Many snake venoms have both neurotoxic and haemotoxic properties. Bites by Neotropical rattlesnakes (the viperid *Crotalus durissus*), for example, cause breathing problems as well as symptoms more typical of viper envenomation, while victims of bites from the black-necked spitting cobra (the elapid *Naja nigricollis*) often suffer serious local tissue damage.

The toxicity of venom is normally measured by calculating the LD_{50} (50% lethal dose), which is the amount required to kill half of the animals (normally mice) into which it is injected. These numbers provide a general indication of how dangerous the venoms of different snakes may be, but in specific terms they show little correlation with the actual clinical danger of any given species to humans after a bite. Calculations of the LD_{50} value in such viperid and elapid snakes as saw-scaled vipers, the bushmaster, kraits and even the black mamba, for example, look pretty innocuous on paper, whereas researchers know from clinical experience that these are among the most dangerous snakes, with high fatality rates. Furthermore, snake venoms differ considerably in their effect on different animals. The African meerkat, for example, which weighs only about 600 g (21 oz), is, weight-for-weight, one thousand times more resistant to the venom of the Cape cobra, *Naja nivea*, than a sheep! It thus seems clear that the only really useful way of learning about the lethal potential of any snake species is by studying a good cross-section of clinical cases in humans.

ABOVE Eastern green mamba, *Dendroaspis angusticeps*, an African member of the elapid family, characterized by the possession of predominantly neurotoxic venoms.

Snake venoms serve two principal purposes: to incapacitate prey and to begin and aid digestion. They consist of various enzymes and other proteins and are among the most complex of all biological toxins. More than 30 different enzymes have been identified from snake venoms, although not all of these are found in the venom of any one species. Some, such as phospholipase A2, are particularly widespread enzymes found in the venom of many species, while others are specialities restricted to smaller groups. For example, the venom of stiletto snakes (atractaspidine lamprophiids of the genus *Atractaspis*) contains a series of unique amino-acid peptides, named sarafotoxins, that have the specific effect of constricting blood vessels and are not known in other snake venoms. Venom composition varies considerably, not just among species, but among populations of the same species, and even within the life of an individual. As juveniles, Brazilian lanceheads (the crotaline viperid *Bothrops moojeni*), for example, feed on frogs and lizards, whereas adults eat small mammals, and this change in dietary habits as they grow larger is accompanied by a corresponding change in venom toxicity. Some snakes have subtly different venoms among different individuals of the same species. This is not well understood, but might be linked to differences in diet and/or natural variation across large geographic ranges.

Various animals that prey on venomous snakes have some degree of natural resistance to their venom. Mongooses are well known for their ability to survive bites from cobras, and the tayra, a Central American member of the weasel family, is able to withstand large doses of the venom of the terciopelo (the crotaline viperid *Bothrops asper*). The common mussurana, *Clelia clelia*, a large dipsadine colubrid snake from Central and South America, is immune to the venom of pit vipers on which it often feeds. In Asia a recently discovered antitoxic factor in the blood of the reticulated python, *Broghammerus reticulatus*, suggests that this snake is at least partially resistant to the bite of Russell's viper, *Daboia russelli*.

Snake venoms are routinely collected for the production of antivenoms, and their potential medical applications have increasingly become the subject of high-investment research. Captotril (Capoten), a multi-million-dollar drug recently developed for treating high blood pressure, for example, is based on a component originally found in the venom of the jararaca, *Bothropoides jararaca*, a South American pit viper.

Among living vertebrate animals, a few small groups of mammals (the platypus and some insectivores) have venom, but the vast majority of venomous vertebrate species are snakes. Recently it has been discovered that among squamate reptiles venom actually evolved before snakes first appeared and it was present already in the most recent common ancestor of snakes and anguimorph lizards. These venoms and the morphological features adapted to deliver it into prey are much less sophisticated in lizards, and the venom has been reduced or lost in many species, one notable exception being the Central and North American Gila monster, *Heloderma suspectum*. Many of the advanced features of snake venom evolved only after snake evolution was well underway, and it might have been one of the factors behind colubroid snakes diversifying into so many species. Venom is formed from a complex mixture of molecules and it can be a substantial drain on the resources of an animal. Thus, it is unsurprising that the ability to make potent venom has been lost in many colubroid snakes that have evolved different behaviours or diets; for example, in several egg- and snail-eating snakes, and in constricting rat snakes (colubrine colubrids). However, a neurotoxin similar to that of elapids has been found in at least one non-venomous colubrine colubrid (*Coelognathus radiatus*). Detailed studies of the molecular biology and evolution of snake venoms are in their infancy and there is still much to learn.

LEFT Vipers, such as the dusky lancehead *Bothriopsis pulchra*, from the eastern slopes of the Andes of South America typically have venoms that are haemotoxic in nature.

REPRODUCTION

Most snakes are oviparous, reproducing by laying eggs, although approximately a quarter of all species are viviparous, giving birth directly to young. Viviparity is sometimes commonly called 'live-bearing' but this is not the best term because eggs also contain live embryos. Sometimes, both kinds of reproduction occur within a single species in different parts of its range. In many snakes males are more abundant than females, but there are at least two species in which the entire population appears to consist only of females. These snakes reproduce without males by means of parthenogenesis ('virgin birth'), and the young snakes are born as miniature clones of their mothers (see p.42).

COURTSHIP AND COPULATION

In almost all snakes there is a pattern of courtship that precedes mating, and while details vary between different species, in most (and the best studied) species it tends to involve the same general sequence of events. The male, which is almost always the more active partner, searches out a receptive female by following the scent trail that she produces from special glands as she moves around. Once he has located her, he approaches and proceeds to work his way gradually forwards over her body with rapid, quivering movements, at the same time rubbing his chin along her back and flicking his tongue in and out constantly. In many pythons and boas the male uses the claw-like vestiges of his hindlimbs to scratch or stroke the female's skin, which appears to have the same stimulative effect. When he reaches the nape of her neck, the male then manoeuvres himself into a mating position by throwing a loop of his body over the lower part of her back and entwining his tail around the opening of her cloaca (the common chamber of the reproductive and digestive tract). If the female is receptive, she responds by raising her tail slightly and opening her cloaca, then the male everts one of his paired hemipenes and copulates with her.

Mating can be a protracted affair, and the male and female may remain joined together for many hours. The duration of copulation might be determined partly by the morphology of the male hemipenis and the number of males a single female will mate with each breeding season. In species in which females are likely to mate with multiple males, copulation is often longer and the males can insert a secretion immediately after sperm transfer that forms a 'copulatory plug' in the female reproductive tract that reduces the likelihood of insemination by other males.

In some species, the female may be surrounded by considerable numbers of males, which in their impassioned attempts to mate with her and 'squeeze' out competing rivals will often entwine themselves together in a large, jumbled mass. Herpetologists have observed this 'balling' behaviour in various different snakes, especially aquatic forms such as anacondas (*Eunectes*), green water snakes (the natricine colubrid *Nerodia cyclopion*), Arafura Asian/Australasian file snakes (the acrochordid *Acrochordus arafurae*), and some sea snakes. A breeding ball of

ABOVE A pair of smooth snakes, the colubrine colubrid *Coronella austriaca*, mating in southern Britain.

anacondas may consist of more than 10 males, all coiled around a single female, and they will stay knotted together like this for up to four weeks. Fertilization may not necessarily happen immediately after mating. Sperm can survive in the female reproductive tract for long periods, and there are instances where the females of some species in captivity have been kept away from males for several years and then unexpectedly given birth to healthy offspring.

Soon after emerging from their winter dens, most males of the North American natricine colubrid *Thamnophis sirtalis parietalis* temporarily produce female pheromones that attract other males and switch off male courting behaviour. These transvestite or she-male snakes appear to benefit from this female-mimicking behaviour by conserving energy resources that have been reduced during overwintering. Later in the season the males produce typical male pheromones and use their increased energy levels to begin mating.

RITUALISTIC COMBAT

Should they encounter each other during the breeding season, the males of many species become aggressive and perform ritualistic combat 'dances'. These competitions take place between adult males of the same species, and usually between individuals that are similarly matched in size. When two such rivals meet, they rise up vertically against each other and entwine their bodies like a twisted rope, each attempting to dominate the other by pushing him over. The display is frequently accompanied by exaggerated swaying movements as each snake attempts to knock the other off balance, and finally ends when the weaker opponent concedes by dropping to the ground and moving away.

Ritualistic combat dances have been observed in species as widely different as American indigo snakes (the colubrine colubrid *Drymarchon corais*), European vipers (*Vipera*), black mambas (the elapid *Dendroaspis polylepis*) in Africa, and Australian tiger snakes (the elapid *Notechis*). Essentially, they amount to little more than a vigorous test of strength, and, except in a few species in which a frustrated male may bite his rival, neither snake usually inflicts serious injury on the other. So preoccupied can a male become in his battle for supremacy that he may become completely oblivious to what is happening around him; a male European adder, *Vipera berus*, for example, will sometimes continue to 'dance' in this way even when its rival has been removed and replaced with a stick.

BELOW Male combat in the western diamondback rattlesnake, the crotaline viperid *Crotalus atrox*, photographed in October in the Tucson Mountains, Arizona, USA.

EGGS AND HATCHING

Eggs are usually laid several weeks or months after mating, and they vary greatly in number according to species and, in many cases, the size of the parent female. Most of the smaller kinds of snakes, such as scolecophidians and some invertebrate-eating members of the Colubridae, typically produce only two or three eggs that in comparison with their body sizes are enormous, while large pythons may lay up to 100 relatively small eggs. Viviparous species in particular often give birth to large numbers of offspring; the record is held by a puff adder, *Bitis arietans*, which produced 156 young in a single litter.

The female snake usually deposits her eggs underground or in a shallow hole on the surface covered with leaves, where they are concealed from predators and insulated from fluctuations in temperature and humidity. The incubation temperature and moisture level to which the eggs are exposed have a direct bearing on their development, and it is thus vitally important that she selects her nest site very carefully. A temperature increase of only a few degrees can halve the time required for the eggs to hatch, while if the nest area becomes too hot or does not retain enough heat the developing embryos within the eggs will perish. In a particularly suitable place, females may deposit their eggs communally and even return to the same site year after year. Favourite nesting sites of the grass snake (the natricine colubrid *Natrix natrix*) in Britain, for example, are garden compost heaps; as these decompose, they generate a good deal of heat, providing an ideal environment for incubation.

Although most snakes leave the nest site and have nothing further to do with the eggs once they are laid, the females of certain kinds, particularly pythons, some elapids (notably the king cobra) and a number of tropical vipers, remain with their clutch during the entire incubation period. Female pythons are unusual in also being able to control the temperature at which their eggs develop (see p.52). The time that elapses before the eggs hatch varies greatly among species; in some snakes hatching may occur only a few days after the eggs have been laid, while in others it may take more than three months. At hatching time, the young snakes break through the leathery shell using a small egg-tooth attached to the end of their snouts, and this is discarded shortly afterwards. The young of viviparous snakes are born enclosed within a membranous sac, which ruptures soon after birth.

PREDATOR EVASION AND DEFENCE

Snakes show a wide range of behaviour in response to predators and the defensive repertoires of some species are elaborate. Almost invariably, however, a snake's first reaction when confronted with danger is to try to escape observation, either by remaining motionless or withdrawing out of sight. Most species are coloured and patterned in a way that conceals them in their natural habitat, reducing the risk of detection by predators and helping them stay hidden from potential prey;

ABOVE Snakes that rely on immobility to evade detection have complex colour patterns that serve to break up the outline of the body and often resemble dead leaves, moss, bark etc. such as this eyelash palm pit viper, *Bothriechis schlegelii*, Costa Rica.

this is known as procrypsis. The complex geometrical markings of Gaboon vipers, *Bitis gabonica*, for example, are extremely effective in disguising these large African snakes among fallen leaves on the forest floor, while the mottled green patterns of some palm pit vipers (*Bothriechis*) are perhaps unsurpassed in concealing these species among the greenery of tropical American rainforests. In addition to having camouflage colour patterns, snakes often have a micro-ornamentation on their exposed body scales that absorbs or scatters rather than reflecting light, so that they do not appear obviously shiny. A number of tree-living specialists in the Colubridae are distinctive in having long, thin bodies that resemble vines, and some, such as those of the genus *Oxybelis*, also have the habit of moving with an irregular swaying action, mimicking a vine or branch trembling in the breeze.

Some snakes do not rely on camouflage but instead appear to try to confuse predators. For example, some crotaline viperids hide their heads, thrash, or raise loops of their body off the ground ('body bridging') when confronted by snake-eating king snakes (the North American colubrine colubrid *Lampropeltis getula*). Species of the Neotropical colubrine colubrid *Chironius* can stiffen the whole of their extended body into a series of short zigzags when disturbed.

LEFT False coral snakes, the Central American dipsadine colubrid *Pliocercus elapoides*, have exceptionally long, fragile tails which are easily broken and thus provide the snake with more than one chance of escape.

WARNING COLORATION

In contrast to colour patterns that provide concealment, those of some snakes draw attention and warn predators of their owners' harmful character. Aposematic (warning) colour patterns, as they are known, are exhibited also by a number of mostly harmless 'mimic' species, which are assumed to derive protection from them in much the same way (see p.94).

BELOW Coral snakes have bright colour patterns that appear to be instinctively avoided by many predators. Similar markings are also seen in a number of harmless 'mimic' species. For example, compare this Maya coral snake, the Central American elapid *Micrurus hippocrepis*, with the false coral snake (above).

ESCAPE

Should their initial attempts to avoid discovery fail, most snakes will try to make good their escape by fleeing. Many of the long, slender terrestrial species in particular are highly agile and when confronted with danger will disappear with a burst of great speed. A startled pink-tailed forest racer (the Neotropical colubrine colubrid *Dendrophidion nuchale*), for example, will dash across the forest floor for 20 m (65 ft) or more before stopping, and these whip-like Central American colubrine snakes may also escape by flinging themselves spectacularly off high rocky outcrops. The 'flying' snakes (the colubrine colubrid genus *Chrysopelea*) of South and Southeast Asia have an even more impressive way of avoiding danger. These accomplished climbers will throw themselves off the highest branches and, with their bodies flattened, glide down to the ground or a lower branch.

TAIL BREAKAGE AND POKING

The ability of a species to voluntarily cast off its tail (autotomy) to escape a predator is most commonly associated with lizards, but there are also several snakes in which this behaviour has arisen. Whereas the broken tail of many lizards will grow back, snakes cannot regenerate their tails. The mechanism of tail breakage in snakes is also different from that in lizards; in most lizards the break occurs directly across a single vertebral segment, whereas in snakes it occurs between vertebrae. In some snakes tail loss is limited to a single breakage, with no further breaks occurring after the initial one, whereas the mechanism in others, such as the Neotropical neck-banded snake, *Scaphiodontophis annulatus*, and the harlequin snake, *Pliocercus elapoides*, of Central America, both colubrine colubrids, appears more specialized.

Instead of sacrificing their tail, other snakes use them to poke into a potential predator that has picked them up. A pointed and hard tail tip increases the effectiveness of this and can make it feel more like a bite. This behaviour is seen in a diverse range of snakes, including typhlopid scolecophidians, uropeltid pipe snakes and atractaspidine lamprophiids (stiletto snakes).

INTIMIDATION DISPLAYS

Many snakes resort to hissing when confronted with danger and various species are known to use other sounds as a means of discouraging unwanted attention. The audible threat displays of rattlesnakes produced by the rapid vibration of their tail rattles are particularly impressive. Neotropical lancehead vipers (*Bothrops*) do not have rattles, but many of these species and several others are able to generate similar sound effects by vibrating their tails among dry leaves. Saw-scaled vipers (*Echis*) and desert horned vipers, *Cerastes cerastes*, produce a rasping sound by rubbing their coarsely keeled body scales together, while western hook-nosed snakes (the colubrid *Gyalopion canum*) and Sonoran coral snakes (the elapid *Micruroides euryxanthus*) are noted for the curious 'popping' sounds they make by drawing air in through the cloaca and expelling it forcibly.

LEFT Should their initial attempts at escape fail, many snakes resort to intimidation tactics when confronted with danger. The startle and threat display of the Asian lined rat snake, the colubrine colubrid *Coelognathus radiatus*, is particularly demonstrative.

BELOW LEFT The Eastern bandy-bandy, *Vermicella annulata*, an Australian elapid that raises loops of its body off the ground to deter predators.

Several snakes make threats with their body posture instead of with sound. Stiletto snakes (species of the atractaspidine lamprophiid *Atractaspis*) press their heads to the ground while arching their necks. Some tree-dwelling colubrid snakes, including Neotropical bird snakes (*Pseustes*), the Australian tree snake, *Dendrelaphis punctulatus*, and the African vine/twig snakes (*Thelotornis*) and boomslang, *Dispholidus typus*, respond to threats by expanding the neck to appear larger. Many snakes also open their mouths wide when alarmed, and some, such as species of the colubrine colubrids *Oxybelis* (Central America), *Philothamnus* (Africa) and *Boiga* (Asia), reveal a strikingly contrasting colour when they gape.

PASSIVE RESISTANCE

When other lines of defence have all been exhausted, some snakes resort to various passive forms of behaviour. Several roll themselves into balls, and some will try to confuse an enemy further by raising and waving their short stumpy tails to imitate a moving head; to add to the illusion, the tails of some species are patterned to resemble the head. Asian sand boas, *Eryx tataricus*, for example, have tail markings that consist of a short, dark, horizontal line and a small spot, resembling the mouth and eye.

RIGHT Cobras, like this southern African *Naja annulifera*, are noted for their upright hooded threat and defense posture.

Another odd form of passive resistance is that used by, among others, the North American hog-nosed snake (the dipsadine colubrid *Heterodon*). When molested, these snakes turn over onto their backs and, after a few convulsive wriggles, lie still with their mouths open and tongues hanging out, as though dead. If the 'lifeless' snake is turned over onto its belly again, however, it gives the game away by promptly rolling back. Even more remarkable is the autohaemorrhaging behaviour of wood snakes (the dwarf 'boa' *Tropidophis*) (see p.71).

As a further deterrent, some Asian natricine colubrids (*Macropisthodon* and some species of *Rhabdophis*) produce a sticky, bitter-tasting substance from neck glands when provoked, and many other snakes will smear themselves with either obnoxious secretions from musk glands at the base of the tail or the contents of their cloacas. These can be especially foul smelling and the odour often persists for many hours, as anyone who has caught a Eurasian grass snake or North American garter snake will not have failed to notice!.

ABOVE Royal or ball pythons, *Python regius*, of Africa are among a number of species that habitually roll themselves up into a tight ball when alarmed.

18	ANOMALEPIDIDAE	
120	LEPTOTYPHLOPIDAE	Scolecophidia
260	TYPHLOPIDAE	
1	ANILIIDAE	
23	TROPIDOPHIIDAE	
3	ANOMOCHILIDAE	
10	CYLINDROPHIIDAE	
50	UROPELTIDAE	
2	BOLYERIIDAE	Henophidia
2	XENOPHIIDAE	
50	BOIDAE	
40	PYTHONIDAE	
1	LOXOCEMIDAE	
2	XENOPELTIDAE	
3	ACROCHORDIDAE	
15	XENODERMATIDAE	
14	PAREATIDAE	
1	Azemiopinae	VIPERIDAE
90	Viperinae	
210	Crotalinae	
40	HOMALOPSIDAE	
350	ELAPIDAE	Colubroidea
21	Atractaspidinae	LAMPROPHIIDAE
50	Aparallactinae	
65	Lamprophiinae	
50	Psammophiinae	
90	Pseudoxyrhophiinae	
680	Colubrinae	COLUBRIDAE
210	Natricinae	
750	Dipsadinae	
90	Calamariinae	

Alethinophidia · Caenophidia

PART TWO

The evolutionary tree and classification of snakes

BIOLOGICAL CLASSIFICATIONS ARE SYSTEMS for arranging the diversity of life. These filing systems help humans to communicate about organisms, but they can also contain information about how life evolved and is interrelated. In evolutionary diversification, new species can arise when ancestral species split, mostly when populations are separated by different distributions/anatomies/behaviours to an extent that becomes too great for them to be held together as a single genetic lineage. This mostly divergent, branching nature of evolution produces a hierarchical pattern of relationships among different groups of organisms. Thus, humans are apes but we are also mammals, vertebrates and animals. Most biologists agree that the different ranks in classifications (species, genera, families etc.) are arbitrary. This arbitrariness becomes less of an issue if we try to make sure that each unit that we name comprises a 'natural group'. A natural group is a complete lineage – one that includes all of the descendants of a particular ancestor. For example, the non-human great apes (gorilla, chimpanzee, orangutan) are not a natural group because their most recent common ancestor also gave rise to humans. But, the human and non-human great apes together do constitute a natural group (termed the family Hominidae).

Biologists today strive to base classifications on natural groups, and that partly explains why snake classification has undergone several major changes. One of the most important of these changes relates to the group Colubroidea. Previously this comprised three families: Elapidae (cobras, mambas and relatives), Viperidae (vipers) and Colubridae. The latter of these was long used to classify all colubroids that did not fit into either Elapidae or Viperidae (two very distinctive groups). More recently, snake biologists have gained better insights into the number and relationships of major lineages within the old 'Colubridae', and several of these lineages are now recognized as distinct families, some of which are more closely related to vipers and/or elapids than they are to each other. Although with time biologists are likely to agree more on what the natural groups of snakes are, there will still be debate as to which lineages are assigned the status of genus, subfamily or family (the

OPPOSITE A summary of the evolutionary relationships and classification of snakes, indicating the positions of families and subfamilies mentioned in this book. Values in boxes indicate the approximate numbers of species in each group. Only the major colubrid and lamprophiid subfamilies are shown. Small green dots indicate ancestral nodes, with the position of the most recent common ancestor of all living snakes shown by the star. The dotted line indicates uncertainty over inclusion of Asian pipe snakes in Henophidia. Some parts of the evolutionary tree are more certain than others as detailed in the main text.

arbitrary units above the species level), which explains some of the ongoing changes in classification. Much of this change involves moving species between genera or dividing a single genus into several genera, in order to try to make these groups natural.

We are clearly now in an important age of snake discovery – both of new species and of their evolutionary relationships. Undoubtedly the classification used here represents a work-in-progress and it will have changed to some degree by the time the next version of this book is published. The snake classification and framework evolutionary tree used in this book (shown in the figure on p.36) is based on the latest analyses of morphological and DNA data, but new analyses are frequently carried out and new information is continually being discovered. Many species have not yet been studied in enough detail to be included in these analyses and, on top of this, new species of snake are being discovered all the time and have to be accommodated into the changing classification. The fossil record, too, will always continue to improve. Some of the relationships are proving more difficult to resolve than others, so we can expect some further changes to this hypothesis over the next few years. We predict that the main areas likely to change are (1) the relationships among pipe snakes, tropidophiids and the core henophidians (pythons, boas etc.), and (2) the number and interrelationships of major lineages within Colubroidea.

On the framework evolutionary tree, the different groups of living snakes are all shown at the tips of the branches of the tree. Each of the branching points (shown by dots) represents the splitting of the most recent common ancestor of those lineages of living snakes that connect directly to the branching point. The further away from the tips of the tree you look, the further back in time these ancestors would have lived. For example, the most recent common ancestor of vipers and pythons lived further back in time than the most recent common ancestor of vipers and elapids. It is important to realize that the position of a group or particular species on the tree does not mean that it can be identified as 'primitive' or 'advanced'. Members of the group Colubroidea are historically referred to as the 'advanced snakes', but this is a

BELOW The Burmese short-tailed python, *Python kyaiktiyo*, was described as a distinct species as recently as 2011. New species of snakes are being discovered frequently, and have been described at a rate of approximately 35 species per year for the period 2007–2011.

misleading name because all organisms are made up of a mixture of primitive and advanced features. So, although scolecophidians lack fangs and venom, they should not be regarded as 'primitive' snakes. Yes, they might retain some primitive features that have been lost in, for example, vipers (such as remnants of the pelvic girdle), but scolecophidians also have many advanced features adapted for their specialized burrowing and feeding behaviours that are not found in vipers.

It is important also to realize that many common names for snakes do not correspond to natural groups. Common names are often based on snakes' overall appearance or habit and habitat, which more often reflects their general ecology than a classification based on their evolutionary tree. For example, many slender snakes the world over that spend much of their time in trees are called 'tree', 'vine' or 'twig' snakes, and at least two not especially closely related groups of nocturnal snakes with large eyes have been called 'cat' snakes, the Asian colubrine colubrids *Boiga* and close relatives plus several Neotropical dipsadine colubrids. 'Garter' snakes are very different animals in Africa (the elapid *Elapsoidea*) and North America (the natricine colubrid *Thamnophis*), and the name 'water' snake has been applied to several evolutionary disparate groups of aquatic and semi-aquatic snakes. Scientific names can also be confusing because they can change as scientific understanding changes, but they are more precise when attempting to communicate about all different kinds of snakes across the whole world.

ABOVE The lamprophiid *Buhoma procterae* from Tanzania. Lamprophiids were considered a subfamily of Colubridae, but they are now generally recognized as a separate family possibly more closely related to elapids than to 'true' colubrids.

PART THREE

Snake diversity

SCOLECOPHIDIA:
Worm, Blind and Thread Snakes

An examination of the evolutionary tree of living snakes (see p.36) shows that the major group Scolecophidia comprises one half of the primary bifurcation in the tree. This is an ancient group of snakes, as old as all the other snakes put together (Alethinophidia). However, they comprise far fewer species (approximately 400) than alethinophidians (about 2,900 species) and are also less morphologically (at least superficially) and ecologically diverse. All the species in the three scolecophidian families are cylindrical, generally small and narrow, have evenly sized body scales, very short tails, and are burrowers in mostly tropical and subtropical sands and soils. They have small, ventrally positioned mouths, very small eyes that are often not visible externally, and they feed mostly on small social insects (ants and termites) and especially their eggs, larvae and pupae. So different is their appearance it is difficult to appreciate that they belong to the same group of vertebrates as, for example, the huge pythons, and it was once even believed that scolecophidians were not snakes at all.

Although many scolecophidian species are commonly called 'blind snakes', there is no evidence that they completely lack visual function. Admittedly their eyesight is unlikely to be good. Each eye is not covered by its own, circular protective cap (the brille), as in most other snakes, but usually lies beneath an enlarged scale on the side of the head. The seven-striped thread snake (the leptotyphlopid *Siagonodon septemstriatus*) has a distinct pupil and coloured iris, and may have better developed vision than many other scolecophidians, but the eyes of many species are smaller. In some scolecophidians the eyes have been reduced substantially and, although they retain a structured retina and lens, they also lie beneath head scales and might only discriminate light/dark instead of being capable of forming a detailed image.

The evolutionary relationships among the three scolecophidian families is an ongoing matter of debate. The natural history of all but a handful of species is little studied and extremely poorly known. All scolecophidian snakes are probably egg-

OPPOSITE Western diamondback rattlesnake, *Crotalus atrox*, a crotaline viperid of arid habitats in southwestern USA and Mexico.

layers, and except for some anomalepidids have only one oviduct, perhaps an evolutionary consequence of their slender body shape. Clutch size ranges from a single, long and very narrow – 25 x 2.5 mm (1 x ¹/₁₀ in) – egg in the Arabian/Asian leptotyphlopid *Myriopholis blanfordi*, to as many as 60, each about 20 x 10 mm (⁴/₅ x ²/₅ in), in the giant Schlegel's blind snake (the typhlopid *Megatyphlops schlegelii*). The eggs laid by some species are so tiny that in size and shape they resemble a grain of rice. Some species lay eggs that are in a very advanced stage of development and hatch within a few days.

ABOVE *Typhlops angolensis*, a large blind snake found throughout much of tropical Africa.

Among the most unusual of the scolecophidian snakes in its reproductive biology is the Brahminy blind snake, the typhlopid *Ramphotyphlops braminus*, which is believed to be an all-female, parthenogenetic species (i.e. it produces offspring without males). This species is also called the 'flower-pot snake' because of its tendency to hide in the soil of potted plants, by which means it has been accidentally transported by humans to many places. A native of southern Asia, it has now become established in regions as far apart as Madagascar, Japan, Australia, Hawaii, Mexico and southeastern USA.

BELOW *Typhlophis squamosus*, an anomalepidid from northern South America.

FAMILY ANOMALEPIDIDAE

The Anomalepididae includes only about 18 species in four genera (*Anomalepis*, *Helminthophis*, *Liotyphlops*, *Typhlophis*), restricted in distribution to tropical Central and South America. In evolutionary terms, these snakes seem to have retained fewer primitive features than other scolecophidians, and most anomalepidids differ from them in lacking vestiges of a pelvis and several other features of the skeleton. Anomalepidids differ from leptotyphlopids and typhlopids in having teeth on both the lower and upper jaws, and in having more rows of scales around the body. Most species are small, with only a few reaching total lengths of over 30 cm (12 in). Very little is known about their natural history, but the few observations that have been made indicate that they have similar diets and habits to most other scolecophidians. The family Anomalepididae does not have any good common English names.

FAMILY LEPTOTYPHLOPIDAE: Thread/Worm Snakes

This family of about 120 species includes the smallest and the most elongate of all living snakes. They occur primarily in South America and Africa, but extend also into Central and southern North America, Arabia and southwestern Asia. They have been recorded from an exceptionally large range of altitudes, from 76 m (250 ft) below sea level (*Rena humilis* in Death Valley, USA) to more than 3,250 m (10,660 ft) above sea level (*Epictia tricolor* in the Andes of Peru). Until very recently, only two genera were recognized (divided into a somewhat confusing assemblage of species groups), but a recent study of DNA has allowed scientists to tease apart some of the diversity within this old family, and to demarcate 12 genera. Although some leptotyphlopids reach over 45 cm (18 in) in total length, *Tetracheilostoma carlae* from Barbados is the smallest known snake with a maximum length of only a little over 10 cm (4 in). Some leptotyphlopids are extremely elongate, with species of the African genera *Myriopholis*, *Namibiana* and *Rhinoleptus* having body widths that are less than 140th of their total length.

In leptotyphlopids the upper jaws have no teeth and are relatively immobile, while the lower (toothed) jaws are highly flexible and are swung backwards and forwards rapidly to rake in ant and termite eggs/larvae. They eat large numbers of these small prey items in each meal, with this special rapid feeding mechanism, probably an adaptation to help them escape from ant and termite nests before suffering attacks from their soldiers. Texas thread snakes, *Rena dulcis*, and perhaps other species too, are thought to form a physical barrier against the bites of these insects by raising the tips of their body scales. Many scolecophidians (and other snakes) produce distasteful secretions that might also help to deter attacking insects.

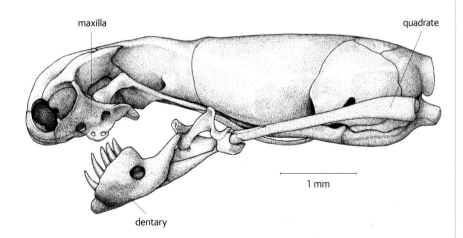

maxilla   quadrate

1 mm

dentary

LEFT Skull of the South American thread snake, *Tricheilostoma macrolepis*. Leptotyphlopids (thread snakes) are unique among snakes in that all of the bones of the upper jaw and palate have lost their teeth. Note the long bone (quadrate) joining the skull to the lower jaw, for pushing the small mouth outwards.

FAMILY TYPHLOPIDAE: Blind Snakes

Typhlopids comprise the largest family of scolecophidians, and the approximately 260 species are also more geographically widespread, occurring in the Americas, Africa, Europe, Asia, Madagascar and Australia. Although they are generally (and here) treated as a single family, a recent DNA study has proposed splitting them into three families (within a new superfamily, Typhlopoidea) because one radiation in Madagascar and one in Asia are genetically very distinct and may have diverged from the other typhlopids much further back in time. Although there are currently only about six genera, there will probably be more named as scientists get to grips with understanding how their diversity is structured.

An African species, Schlegel's blind snake, *Megatyphlops schlegelii*, is the largest known scolecophidian, growing to almost 1 m (3¼ ft) long and about 3 cm (1⅕ in) in diameter. There are several other 'giant' typhlopids that reach lengths of more than 60 cm (24 in), but in general the average length of these snakes is 15–30 cm (6–12 in). All species, including the largest, seem to feed exclusively on small invertebrates. Typhlopids are generally more stocky than leptotyphlopids, but there are a wide range of body shapes. *Ramphotyphlops angusticeps* from the Solomon Islands has a particularly long body with more than 600 individual vertebrae, perhaps the greatest number of any snake (or any other vertebrate). Several typhlopids seem to lack body pigment entirely. In life these species are bright pink thanks to the oxygenated blood in their translucent bodies.

Superficially the heads of typhlopids are like those of leptotyphlopids, but internally there are surprising differences. In almost a complete reverse of the leptotyphlopid condition, the upper jaws have teeth and are freely moving while the lower jaws are toothless and rigidly attached to each other anteriorly. Like the leptotyphlopids they can feed very rapidly (swallowing nearly 100 small prey items in one minute) by raking, but in typhlopids it is the upper jaws that perform this function. *Acutotyphlops subocularis* of New Guinea are unusual in that they feed mostly on earthworms, which are swallowed whole.

ABOVE The typhlopid *Austrotyphlops nigrescens* from Australia.

RIGHT Skull of *Afrotyphlops punctatus*, an African 'blind' snake (Family Typhlopidae). The upper jaw has a couple of teeth, while the lower is toothless. Unlike leptotyphlopids the maxillary bones of the upper jaw are also not rigidly attached to each other but capable of some independent movement.

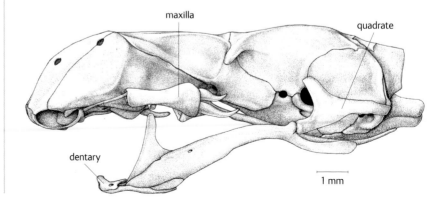

maxilla

quadrate

dentary

1 mm

THREAD SNAKES AND SCREECH OWLS

ABOVE Texas thread snake, the leptotyphlopid *Rena dulcis*.

Eastern screech owls, *Otus asio*, feed mainly on insects, but among the various other small animals that parent birds in southern USA occasionally catch and take back to their nestlings are Texas thread snakes, *Rena dulcis*. Unusually, however, the owls do not always kill the snakes, as they do most other kinds of prey, but carry them back to the nest alive, where apparently many are then released (or escape from the bird's bill and talons) and survive by eating the larvae of parasitic insects. Some captured snakes continue to live in the nest, feeding on insect larvae even after the young owls have fledged.

Infestations of scavenging and parasitic insects often plague the nests of screech owls, and this appears to be one of the main underlying reasons why in parts of their range their broods so often fail. Young owls in nests that contain thread snakes, however, appear to grow faster and suffer lower mortality than do those in which there are no snakes, so evidently there is at least some benefit to the owls in having these live-in cleaners around. It remains to be seen if the occurrence of thread snakes in screech owl nests is merely the result of them having fortuitously escaped being eaten, or if there is some complex, mutually beneficial interaction between these animals at play. Where they occur in other parts of the world, thread snakes are often preyed on by owls and invariably eaten by these birds.

ANILIIDAE, CYLINDROPHIIDAE, ANOMOCHILIDAE AND UROPELTIDAE:
Pipe Snakes and Shieldtails

These snakes generally have elongate, cylindrical bodies, and ventral scales that are weakly differentiated and only slightly wider than the dorsal ones. They have small mouths that cannot be extended to swallow wide prey, and they retain several primitive features that have been lost in most living snake lineages (e.g. a coronoid bone in the lower jaw, see p.12, and in many cases a vestigial pelvic girdle and hindlimbs). For a long time they were considered to represent a single natural group, or a series of groups that all were removed from the main branch of the snake evolutionary tree. However, recent studies, especially of DNA data, have demonstrated that there are two distinct groups involved, one in South America and one in Asia, and that they might not be especially closely related (see p.36).

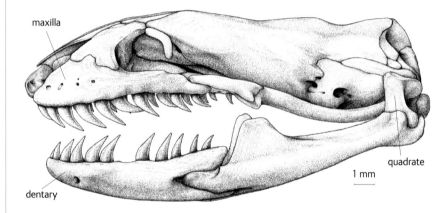

RIGHT Skull of the cylindrophiid pipe snake, *Cylindrophis ruffus*. Pipe snake skulls retain several primitive features for snakes and have only a few large teeth. The snout and jaw bones are not very movably connected to each other or the braincase, as in most other snakes, and the lower jaw, too, is relatively inflexible so that these snakes do not eat wide prey.

maxilla

quadrate

1 mm

dentary

FAMILY ANILIIDAE: Neotropical Pipe Snakes

Aniliidae comprises a single species, *Anilius scytale*, found in the forests of the Amazonian and Guiana Shield regions of South America. This species is sometimes called the false coral snake because of its overall body shape (cylindrical with a short tail and narrow head), partly burrowing lifestyle and exceptionally bold colour pattern. Unlike coral snakes (Family Elapidae), to humans *Anilius* is very mellow and non-venomous. It

BELOW The strikingly marked South American pipe snake, the aniliid *Anilius scytale*, grows up to about 90 cm (3 ft) long.

relies on its warning coloration and body-flattening behaviour to keep predators off. It has very small eyes that lie beneath a relatively large, transparent, polygonal scale. This species retains the primitive feature of teeth on the premaxilla. Although mostly burrowing in habit, it can be found in and near water, and many specimens have been found moving above ground at night. It gives birth to 3–13 young. The narrow-mouthed *Anilius* seems to feed only on long-bodied and narrow prey, including other snakes, caecilians (burrowing, limbless amphibians), amphisbaenians (burrowing, limbless lizards) and eels.

FAMILIES CYLINDROPHIIDAE AND ANOMOCHILIDAE:
Asian Pipe Snakes

Cylindrophiidae is represented by 10 species grouped in the genus *Cylindrophis*, and found across Indochina and the islands of Southeast Asia, with a single species (*C. maculatus*) in Sri Lanka. Sometimes included within the Cylindrophiidae, the single genus and three species in the family Anomochilidae are restricted to peninsular Malaysia and Borneo.

When danger threatens, cylindrophiids can flatten and curl their tails upwards to expose boldly patterned and coloured undersurfaces. The dorsal colour of some species is a uniform brown, while others are marked with black cross-bars and a lengthways stripe along the middle of the back, and all species have black-and-white-chequered bellies. Like other pipe snakes, they are burrowers in loose, wet soil or leaf litter, usually close to the surface. They live in rainforest and wetlands, but some species can also be found in agricultural habitats. As far as is known, they are all viviparous. *Cylindrophis* have been recorded feeding on eels and caecilians, but have also been known to accept small fish in captivity.

Dwarf pipe snakes (*Anomochilus*) are small species, growing to only just over 50 cm (20 in). They are boldly marked with pale spots and two species have bright red bands on the tail. Unlike other pipe snakes, they are egg-layers, although apart from this (and that they live in rainforests) very little is known about their natural history. The diets of *Anomochilus* are unknown, but the small head and body size of these little snakes indicate that they probably eat only narrow prey such as small caecilians and snakes or perhaps worms and other invertebrates.

ABOVE The anomochilid *Anomochilus monticola* from the Mount Kinabalu region of Borneo. Note the slender, cylindrical body and iridescent scales.

LEFT Asian pipe snakes range in length from about 40 cm (16 in) in the Sri Lankan pipe snake, *Cylindrophis maculatus*, to 70 cm (28 in) in this widespread Southeast Asian species, the red-tailed pipe snake, *C. ruffus*.

FAMILY UROPELTIDAE: Shieldtails

The shieldtails, of which there are eight genera (*Brachyophidium*, *Melanophidium*, *Platyplectrurus*, *Plectrurus*, *Pseudotyphlops*, *Rhinophis*, *Teretrurus*, *Uropeltis*) and about 50 species, are a fascinating group of distinctive-looking snakes restricted to Sri Lanka and the Indian peninsula. They spend most of their time burrowing in moist soils, particularly in mountainous regions. They resemble pipe snakes in being cylindrical, feeding on narrow prey and having a robust skull that retains several primitive features. They differ from pipe snakes in having no vestiges of the hindlimbs or a pelvis, and most are also even more radically modified for subterranean life.

Among their various burrowing adaptations is a unique feature that affects the mobility of the head. The anterior vertebrae of the neck have exceptionally flexible joints, allowing the snake to bend its head to an unusually sharp angle. The muscles of the neck and forepart of the body have also become especially well developed for pushing the small, narrow, often very pointed head forcefully through soil. When they are tunnelling, the neck makes a series of regular sideways-directed movements, which widens the burrow through which the snake is moving and allows it to draw the rest of its body up behind.

The most notable feature of shieldtails, and the feature for which they are collectively named, is the oddly shaped end of the tail. In some species this is capped with a spine or has an enlarged, roughened scale, while in others the tail terminates abruptly as a broad, flattened disc covered with many spines or sharp keels. Internally the tail shield is supported by a bony plate. The curiously modified tails of these snakes probably serve some adaptive function in protecting them; when threatened with attack, a shieldtail will tuck its head between or under body coils and wave its tail around, a behavioural trait that probably evolved as a means of diverting a predator's attention away from the snake's more vulnerable head.

Shieldtails are small snakes, about 20–75 cm (8–30 in) in length, with most species towards the lower end of this size range. Some species are brilliantly coloured, with

RIGHT The Indian uropeltid *Uropeltis macrolepis mahableshwarensis*. Note the flattened shield-like form of the tail.

bold red, orange and/or yellow markings, while others are uniformly black. As with many other groups of burrowing snakes, their scales are often highly iridescent. They occur mostly in mountain rainforests and agricultural plots that have replaced this native habitat, although some, such as the monotypic *Pseudotyphlops philippinus* of Sri Lanka, occur in lowland areas. They feed mainly on earthworms, and while burrowing in search of prey they may form deep underground tunnels. Some species can be found in high densities. Although living mostly within the soil, shieldtails can be seen on the surface during and shortly after heavy rains, perhaps to avoid drowning in burrows, but probably also to feed on surface-active earthworms.

LOXOCEMIDAE AND XENOPELTIDAE:
Sunbeam Snakes

Loxocemidae and Xenopeltidae are small families that make up the sunbeam snakes and although widely separated geographically, they are superficially similar and both possibly most closely related to pythons. Their scales have an unusually iridescent quality, particularly those of the Asian *Xenopeltis unicolor*, and for this reason they are often referred to as 'sunbeam snakes'. They are semi-burrowing snakes of moderate size – about 1 m (3¼ ft) in length – and are all egg-layers.

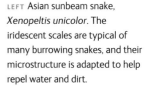

LEFT Asian sunbeam snake, *Xenopeltis unicolor*. The iridescent scales are typical of many burrowing snakes, and their microstructure is adapted to help repel water and dirt.

Loxocemus bicolor from the Neotropics is the sole living representative of the Loxocemidae. Although DNA suggests that it might be the closest living relative of the python family, it was previously variously linked with the pipe snakes of the family Aniliidae and with the Xenopeltidae. It has vestiges of a pelvic girdle, and also the primitive features of supraorbital bones and premaxillary teeth. *Loxocemus* is a constrictor and feeds on lizards and small rodents, largely underground. Turtle and iguana eggs also feature in its diet. Originally described from El Salvador, it occurs also in Mexico and the Pacific lowlands of Central America.

ABOVE Neotropical sunbeam snake, *Loxocemus bicolor*.

The Xenopeltidae is an Old World family with one genus, *Xenopeltis*, and two species, both in Asia. Although separated by millions of years of evolution, among living snakes Xenopeltidae is probably most closely related to Loxocemidae or to Loxocemidae plus Pythonidae. In general appearance they resemble *Loxocemus*, especially in body proportions and the appearance of their scales, and similarly they have a relatively long left lung (approximately half as long as the right lung), premaxillary teeth, and a jaw mechanism that is more flexible than that of pipe snakes. Unlike *Loxocemus*, however, there are no supraorbital bones or evidence of a pelvic girdle. Asian sunbeam snakes have a rather cylindrical body, and the head is somewhat flattened with quite small eyes. They are largely subterranean and/or semi-aquatic in habit. They feed perhaps primarily on snakes, but will also eat small mammals and frogs in captivity. *Xenopeltis unicolor*, the most wide-ranging species, lives in India, southern China, and throughout much of Southeast Asia, including many of the Indonesian and Philippine islands. Its less well-known relative, *X. hainanensis*, appears to occur only in China.

BOIDAE AND PYTHONIDAE: Boas and Pythons

AFFINITIES OF BOAS AND PYTHONS

Although they resemble each other in many features, especially in their adaptations to similar environmental conditions, most researchers now accept that boas and pythons are not quite as closely related as was once believed. Primitive features found in all species are a long row of palatal teeth and a pelvis with vestigial hindlimbs, visible as small claw-like spurs at the base of the tail. Most have a relatively large left lung (typically 30–60% as long as the right lung), and some also have supraorbital bones, premaxillary teeth, and small temperature-sensing pits in, behind or between scales along the lips. The bones of the skull are more loosely articulated than in the mostly burrowing snakes covered in preceding sections, enabling boas and pythons to swallow particularly large prey. Anyone who has observed these snakes feeding

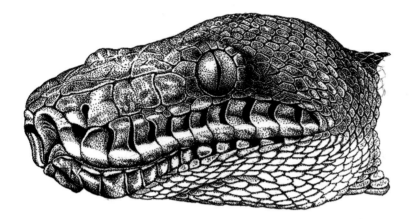

LEFT AND BELOW LEFT The heat sensory organs of boas most typically occur between the labial (lip) scales as exhibited by the emerald tree boa (left). Those of pythons, such as this amethystine python, *Morelia amethistina*, of Indonesia, New Guinea and northern Australia (below left), are generally placed within the labial scales.

cannot fail to be impressed by their extraordinary ability to extend the jaws around what often seems to be an impossibly large mouthful.

Boas and pythons are almost completely mutually exclusive in their geographic distribution. There are no boas in Southeast Asia or Australia, only pythons, of which there are nine species in the former region and just over 20 in the latter. In the Americas and Madagascar, there are only boas. Only in the New Guinea region and parts of India and Africa do the ranges of some species overlap, and in these areas they tend to occupy different habitats. Pythons are distinguished from boas in the arrangement of certain bones of the skull, the placement of their heat-detecting pits and, except for one Australian genus, in having teeth on the premaxilla. Based on thorough analyses of their physical characteristics and DNA, pythons and boas are now thought to represent two distinct lineages and are classified in different families (Pythonidae and Boidae) that might not be each other's closest living relatives.

FAMILY PYTHONIDAE: Pythons

Whereas boas typically give birth to fully formed live young, all python species are oviparous. The females of many pythons are able to incubate their eggs using muscular contractions of the body to generate heat – an unexpected ability for an animal that is otherwise regarded as 'cold-blooded' and incapable of producing metabolic heat. This is achieved by spasmodic contractions of the muscles, which has the effect of increasing the temperature between the female's body and the eggs around which she is coiled. When the ambient air temperature is too low, the female envelops the clutch more tightly within her coils and increases the rate of contractions, or 'twitching', while, if it is too high, she relaxes her body to permit greater ventilation, and twitches less frequently. A female python may stay coiled around her eggs for the entire incubation period (up to three months or more in some species), only leaving them occasionally to drink or bask.

BELOW Children's python, *Antaresia childreni*, of Australia. The females of many python species brood their eggs for up to 3 months or more, during which time they do not feed and may leave only occasionally to bask or drink.

LEFT The African rock python, *Python sebae*, is exceeded in size perhaps only by the reticulated python. Its diet includes animals up to the size of small antelopes, and there are authentic reports of it also having eaten humans.

BELOW Reticulated python, *Broghammerus* (previously *Python*) *reticulatus*. Although primarily terrestrial, this huge Southeast Asian python is also an excellent swimmer and was one of the first vertebrates to re-colonize the volcanic island of Krakatau after its destructive eruption in 1883.

African and Asian pythons

Of four species of python found in Africa, the most widely distributed and by far the largest is the African rock python, *Python sebae*. These huge snakes occur in dry bush country and forests, and, though mostly terrestrial, they climb well and are also semi-aquatic. Among their favourite haunts are river banks, from where they can slip away into the water when danger threatens. The royal python, *P. regius*, of West Africa, and the Angola python, *P. anchietae*, of Angola and the northern half of southwest Africa, are small terrestrial snakes that seldom exceed 2 m (6½ ft) in length. Named for its handsome and clear-cut markings, the royal python is also called the ball python in allusion to its habit of rolling into a tight ball. It occurs mostly in open forests and grasslands, and in parts of its range is quite common, whereas the Angola python is a comparatively rare species apparently more or less confined to rocky habitats.

The fourth species, *P. natalensis,* is distributed across much of southern Africa.

Largest of five Asiatic species is the reticulated python, *Broghammerus reticulatus,* found in much of equatorial Southeast Asia, including the Philippines and parts of the Indonesian archipelago. Although relatively slender, it is longer than other pythons and is probably the world's longest living snake (see p.60). Some individuals may attain lengths over 8 m (26 ft). It occurs in lowland areas, and, although essentially a terrestrial species, it climbs readily and is also often found in water. Along with *B. timoriensis*, this species was previously classified in the genus *Python*, but they have been reclassified into the genus *Broghammerus* because they are more closely related to Australo-Papuan pythons than to the 'typical' *Python* of Africa and Asia. Another large, mostly terrestrial species is the Asian rock python, *P. molurus*, found over much of the Indian subcontinent and also in parts of Southeast Asia. Like the reticulated python it is an opportunistic ambush predator that may also actively forage for prey. Although much smaller, short-tailed pythons are distinctive in having a particularly stout, heavy-set body. Previously regarded as a single species with geographically distinct populations (subspecies), these strikingly marked snakes are more usually now considered four separate species, all similar in body proportions and general habits, but varying in scale features, colour patterns and genetics. Adult Sumatran short-tailed pythons, *P. curtus*, are often dark, whereas the general body colour of the Borneo species (*P. breitensteini*) is more usually a rich yellow-brown. The southern mainland species (*P. brongersmai*) is sometimes bright red. The Burmese species (*P. kyaiktiyo*) has more ventral scales, occurs much further north than any of the other species, and was described only in 2011.

BELOW Sumatran short-tailed python, *Python curtus*. Short-tailed pythons are terrestrial but also spend long periods immersed in muddy swamps or concealed among aquatic vegetation, where they lie in ambush mostly for small mammals.

BEHAVIOURAL SECRETS OF THE WATER PYTHON

ABOVE Australian water python, *Liasis fuscus*.

Owing to their elusive habits, the inherent difficulties of observing them in the wild, and insufficient research effort the natural lives of many snakes remain to a large extent unknown. One of the few species to have been studied in any great detail is the water python, *Liasis fuscus*, an inhabitant of the seasonally flooded grasslands and billabongs (backwater pools) of northern Australia. By implanting some of these pythons with miniature radio transmitters and monitoring their movements (a method known as radiotelemetry) over several years, Australian biologists have been able to build up a detailed picture of their natural history.

These pythons apparently occupy different habitats and feed on different prey depending on the time of year. During the dry season, they spend the days hidden in dense reedbeds, emerging at dusk to feed more or less exclusively on rats that at this time of year live in the numerous deep cracks of the floodplain mud. Having eaten during the night, the snakes make their way back to the same reeds, where they remain until they need another meal. This pattern of activity continues throughout the dry season until the rains arrive and the rats, having all abandoned their homes to escape the rising water levels, are no longer anywhere to be found. At this time the snakes move out into the spreading floodwaters, where they become more or less completely aquatic and switch to feeding on water birds and their eggs. Throughout the wet season they live in these shallow billabongs, concealed among the waterweed and surrounded by literally thousands of plovers, ducks and other breeding birds.

This ability of water pythons to make use of different resources depending on local conditions is impressive in itself, but an unforeseen event that occurred during the biologists' study inadvertently revealed an even greater flexibility in their behaviour. One of the billabongs that the pythons used as a daytime retreat was emptied for a while to control introduced waterweeds. Deprived of their usual habitat and food supply, the snakes survived by moving away and foraging for prey in the surrounding woodlands, even climbing high into trees, where they remained until the billabong eventually refilled.

Macklot's python, *Liasis mackloti*, a large semi-aquatic species from Indonesia, Papua New Guinea, and coastal northern Australia.

Australian and New Guinea pythons

Many different pythons are widely distributed in Australia, New Guinea and the many archipelagos in this region. Among those from Australia, four species of *Antaresia* are small snakes that rarely exceed 1.5 m (5 ft), and at less than 50 cm (20 in) long, the pygmy python, *A. perthensis*, from the western Pilbara region is the smallest of all pythons. Two other Australian pythons, comprising the genus *Aspidites*, differ from all others in lacking externally visible heat-detecting pits. The woma, *A. ramsayi*, occurs in arid habitats throughout much of the continent, while the black-headed python, *A. melanocephalus*, is known mostly from northern Australia. These snakes mainly eat reptiles, including other snakes.

Largest of the pythons of the Australo–Papuan region is Kinghorn's python, *Morelia kinghorni*, found in northeast Australia and nearby islands. Another Australian 'giant', found only on the dry sandstone escarpments of Arnhem Land in Northern Territory, is the Oenpelli python, *M. oenpelliensis*, famed for having remained undiscovered by scientists until the late 1970s. Adults may attain lengths

THE REMARKABLE PHYSIOLOGY OF PYTHONS

It is well known that several pythons are able to consume enormous prey relative to their body size (see p.60), a useful adaptation for animals that only feed rarely. Because these snakes generally wait for their prey to come to them, they may have to go for long periods of time (up to several months) without feeding. In between meals energy is scarce and pythons have developed an amazing physiology that is able to save valuable energy during periods of fasting yet maximize the use of food resources when they appear or are needed. A recent study of the Burmese python, *Python molurus bivittatus*, has shown that while waiting for its next prey item, the digestive and blood circulatory systems are vastly reduced in size, structure and function. The stomach, pancreas and gall bladder do not produce or secrete their usual chemicals, enzyme activity is depressed and the intestine becomes greatly reduced. Even the heart, liver and kidneys have a much reduced mass.

What is perhaps most startling, however, is the speed with which the dormant viscera are able to resume their normal function after a prey item has been caught. A rapid response is essential because a swallowed prey carcass would otherwise soon rot if it is not digested. In just 24 hours, acid production by the stomach has reduced the pH from neutral (pH 7) to very acidic (pH 2). This dissolves the meal, so that by day 3 all that is left of a mammal is some vertebrae and clumps of hair. In preparation for this broken down matter (chyme) from the stomach, the microvilli (tiny finger-like projections on the walls) of the small intestine (which take up nutrients into the bloodstream) grow at an impressive rate, doubling in length in the first six hours. The mass of the small intestine itself increases by 70% within 24 hours of feeding. After six or seven days the system begins to down-regulate once more, also with impressive speed. In total the python's liver and kidneys can double in size and breathing and heartbeat output increase five-fold while digesting. Strangely, even this large increase in breathing is not sufficient to meet the increase in gas exchange required to fuel digestion and so the snake hypoventilates during this period.

The benefit of largely shutting down the gastrointestinal system when no food is available is having a much reduced metabolic rate, which means that less precious energy is expended. Snake species that shut down their digestive systems in this way show an almost 50% reduction in metabolic rate when compared with species that feed more regularly and maintain a similar level of activity in their guts when fasting.

of over 5 m (16 ft), and can overpower prey up to the size of a small wallaby. The Australian olive python, *Liasis olivaceous*, reaches a similar size and regularly eats wallabies. From the lowland monsoon forests and flooded savannas of New Guinea, the Papuan python, *Apodora papuana*, is a similarly large species, while Boelen's python, *Morelia boeleni*, also found only in New Guinea, is one of the most rarely seen of all pythons. This spectacular-looking snake is black with an overlying purple-blue sheen and a series of bright yellow diagonal streaks. Almost nothing is known of its habits in the wild, other than it occurs in highland forests above 1,000 m (3,300 ft).

Among various other pythons from the Australo–Papuan region, D'Albertis python, *Leiopython albertisii*, is a terrestrial species of lowland rainforests in New Guinea, the green tree python, *Morelia viridis*, is an exclusively arboreal, green snake remarkably similar in appearance to a species of boa in South America (see p.67), and the Timor python, *Broghammerus timoriensis*, is a large, semi-arboreal species possibly restricted to the island of Flores.

RIGHT Common boas, *Boa constrictor*, are among the largest snakes in tropical America, although even large specimens, such as this 3 m (10 ft) long example at the side of a forest track, are not easy to see.

FAMILY BOIDAE: True Boas

Boa constrictors

Perhaps the most familiar of all the snakes in this group is the common boa constrictor, *Boa constrictor*. Now considered to be the only species in the *Boa* genus, this tropical American species has one of the largest geographic distributions of any boid, ranging from Mexico in the north and throughout Central and northern South America into Argentina in the south, and it also occurs in a wide variety of habitats. Common boas are large and heavy-bodied, and although they were long believed to have reached a length of 5.6 m (18½ ft), they rarely seem to grow larger than 3.6 m (12 ft).

African and Madagascan boas

Three species from Madagascar were once included in the genus *Boa*, but have now been placed in other genera. The Madagascan ground boa, *Acrantophis madagascariensis*, and Dumeril's ground boa, *A. dumerili*, are heavy-bodied terrestrial species that attain lengths of approximately 2 m (6½ ft), while *Sanzinia madagascarensis* is a slightly smaller and more slender tree-dweller.

BELOW Dumeril's ground boa, *Acrantophis dumerili*, is one of three boa species restricted to Madagascar.

Probably the closest living relative of the Madagascan boas, the Calabar boa, *Calabaria reinhardtii*, inhabits forested regions of West Africa. Because of its habit of laying eggs, this unusual snake was long thought to be related to pythons and only recently have biologists found evidence (particularly from DNA) suggesting it has closer affinities with boas. When threatened with danger, Calabar boas tend to raise the tail to divert attention away from the head, keeping the latter tucked safely beneath their body coils. They may also roll themselves into a tight ball and release a potent musky scent from special anal glands.

Anacondas

Another famous group of boas are the anacondas (*Eunectes*) of which the green anaconda, *E. murinus*, is arguably the largest (but not longest) snake in the world (see p.60). This truly enormous species has a wide distribution over much of tropical South America. A smaller species, the yellow anaconda, *E. notaeus*, occurs in southern parts of the Amazon basin and one other species, the dark-spotted anaconda, *E. deschauenseei*, lives on the island of Marajó in the mouth of the Amazon. Anacondas are highly aquatic boas in which the eyes and nostrils are on top of the head, and they are almost always found in or near to water, especially swamps and slow-moving rivers. They are mostly ambush-hunters and feed on a wide range of prey. In the seasonally flooded llanos (grassy plains) of Venezuela, green anacondas conceal themselves beneath dense floating mats of water hyacinth, from where they lunge at prey as large as the sheep-sized capybaras and occasionally small caimans.

Tree boas

Seven species of tree boas, *Corallus*, are a specialized group of tree-dwellers with relatively slender bodies flattened from side to side, long prehensile tails, and very long mandibular teeth. All found in the Neotropics, four of these are members of the common tree boa species complex (a group of similar organisms that probably represent an undetermined number of truly different species), two (*C. hortulanus* and *C. ruschenbergerii*) occur on the South American mainland, while the others are found on the Caribbean islands of St Vincent (*C. cookii*), and Grenada (*C. grenadensis*). Cropani's boa, *C. cropanii*, may be one of the rarest snakes in the world (see p.62).

Tree boas are nocturnal snakes that use both active and ambush hunting methods to catch their prey. In terms of food preferences, the least specialized is the common tree boa, *C. hortulanus*, which eats frogs, lizards, birds and small mammals, including bats. Emerald tree boas, *C. caninus*, and annulated tree boas, *C. annulatus*, are relatively stout-bodied snakes that show a strong preference for rodents and other endothermic prey. Where

BELOW A new-born emerald tree boa, *Corallus caninus*. As these snakes mature their colour pattern gradually changes to bright green (see p. 67).

prey is abundant, Grenada tree boas in particular may be relatively common. Some of the densest populations of this species are found in or next to fruit orchards, where they feed on the lizards and small mammals that can thrive in these areas.

GIANT SNAKES

'There lay in the mud and water, covered with flies, butterflies and insects of all sorts, the most colossal anaconda which ever my wildest dreams had conjured up. Ten or twelve feet of it lay stretched out on the bank in the mud. The rest of it lay in the clear, shallow water, one huge loop of it under our canoe, its body as thick as a man's waist. It measured fifty feet for certainty, and probably nearer sixty'.

ABOVE Green anaconda, *Eunectes murinus*, at Ilha Caviana on the Amazon River, Brazil.

So wrote an explorer (F W Up de Graff, in *Head Hunters of the Amazon*, 1923) of an encounter in Amazonian Ecuador with a monster anaconda – probably greatly exaggerated because there are no reliable records of snakes greater than 8.7 m (28½ ft) in length. Although possibly not the longest snake in the world, the green anaconda, *Eunectes murinus*, is certainly the most massive. Most early references to 'giant' anacondas and pythons appear to have been grossly exaggerated or based on the length of the removed skin, which is easily stretched. For example, the longest known anaconda is often reported to be 11.4 m (37½ ft), found in eastern Colombia during the 1930s, but the accuracy of this measurement has been doubted and truly reliable records indicate that the maximum size attained by these snakes is closer to 8 m (26 ft).

Another 'giant' is the reticulated python, *Broghammerus reticulatus*, of Southeast Asia. This species is also claimed to attain lengths of 9 m (30 ft) or more, though it does not rival the sheer girth and bulk of its South American relative. The most reliable documented length for a reticulated python is for an individual appropriately named 'Colossus', that lived for many years at the Pittsburgh Zoo in Pennsylvania, USA;

it measured 8.7 m (28½ ft) and weighed 145 kg (320 lb). Almost as controversial as the size attained by anacondas and the larger species of python are tales about what they reputedly eat. In parts of South America, for example, anacondas are often held responsible for the unexplained disappearance of horses and oxen, and in Africa large rock pythons, *Python sebae*, are believed by some to prey on buffalo. In 1952 a Sri Lankan newspaper even carried an article describing a python (presumably *Python molurus*) attacking a baby elephant. While such stories seem outrageous, and are probably based on little more than hearsay and fabrication, these snakes are nonetheless capable of consuming enormous meals. One genuine case concerns a 5.5 m (18 ft) Asian rock python that, having been discovered with a huge bulge in its stomach, was found to have eaten a full-grown leopard. They need a remarkable physiology to process such huge meals (see p.57).

Although today's anacondas and pythons can grow to impressive sizes, they would be dwarfed by some of the extinct snakes known only from fossil remains. The largest snake ever known to have lived is the anaconda-like *Titanoboa cerrejonensis* (see p.9), fossils of which were discovered in Colombia from rocks approximately 60 million years old. This colossal snake is estimated to have reached a length of at least 13 m (43 ft) and a mass of more than 1,000 kg (2,200 lb). The climate must have been notably warmer at that time for snakes to have reached this size.

Rainbow and Caribbean boas

Nine species of boa in the genus *Epicrates* are variously distributed among the islands of the Caribbean. A tenth, named the rainbow boa, *Epicrates cenchria*, with a vast range in Latin America, has recently been split into five distinct species. The Argentine rainbow boa, *E. alvarezi*, is the most genetically distinct of this group and is found in the Argentine and Bolivian Chaco, while the brown rainbow boa, *E. maurus*, inhabits dry forests from Nicaragua to northern Brazil.

At a length of more than 3 m (10 ft), *E. angulifer* from Cuba is by far the largest *Epicrates*, and three other species, *E. inornatus* (Puerto Rico), *E. subflavus* (Jamaica) and *E. striatus* (Bahamas, Hispaniola), also grow quite large. These snakes are semi-arboreal in habit and feed on a wide variety of prey. Cuban and Puerto Rican boas in particular are known for their habit of catching bats as they emerge at dusk from cave entrances. Among the five smaller species, Haitian vine boas, *E. gracilis*, occur in lowland woods near water, whereas the Mona Island boa, *E. monensis*, is found in dry habitats. Pregnant females of this species have been found in termite nests and may use these sun-baked places for regulating their body temperature.

LEFT The Cuban boa, *Epicrates angulifer*, is an inhabitant mostly of forested areas and, although typically found in trees, is equally at home on the ground.

BELOW LEFT Rainbow boa, *Epicrates cenchria*, from tropical South America, Paraguay and Argentina.

ENDANGERED RARITIES

LEFT Cropani's boa, *Corallus cropani*.

Among these is Cropani's boa, *Corallus cropanii*, which is represented by perhaps no more than three specimens in museum collections, all of which have originated from the vicinity of the type locality (the site from which the original specimen was described) near Miracatu in the State of São Paulo, Brazil. Virtually nothing is known about its natural history other than that it occurs in the Atlantic rainforests at 40–45 m (130–150 ft) above sea level. Herpetologists do not know why it is so rare. Although it is restricted to a much diminished habitat, there is still a good deal of intact and protected Atlantic forest remaining in São Paulo State. There is also a long history of local people in Brazil, and especially São Paulo State, bringing any snakes encountered to the Instituto Butantan research centre in São Paulo, and even today this institute receives many snakes from the general range of Cropani's boa every year. Given the level of encroachment on the area during forest clearance and agricultural work it is rather surprising that more specimens have not come to light. Whether or not this elusive boa still survives remains a mystery.

Snakes may be rare in the wild for a variety of reasons. Their numbers may be affected, for example, by habitat destruction, exploitation by the leather and pet animal trades, or through their use as food. One species that has suffered at the hands of human activities is the Antiguan racer (the dipsadine colubrid *Alsophis antiguae*). This snake became extinct on the Caribbean island of Antigua, and its demise seems to have been caused by mongooses released in the late nineteenth century to kill snakes in farmers' fields. On neighbouring Great Bird Island the snake does remain, but even here the population was reduced to a mere 50 individuals in 1995, in this case because of non-native black rats that reached the island on ships. Fortunately this story is a positive one, thanks to the combined efforts of six conservation groups and a team of dedicated volunteers. By removing black rats from Great Bird and 11 other islands, as well as starting up a captive breeding programme, numbers of what was once considered the 'world's rarest snake' increased ten-fold to 500 in 2010. The team even introduced the snake to some adjacent islands and its range now includes an extra 63 hectares beyond Great Bird Island. The conservation effort has done more than just help the Antiguan racer, because populations of birds, turtles and lizards are also increasing thanks to the removal of black rats.

There are other species that seem to have always been extremely scarce even in pristine, undisturbed habitat.

A distinction needs to be drawn between species that are truly rare, and those that are rarely encountered by humans (especially scientists) because of the region and/or habitat in which they live. We do not know the actual abundance of the vast majority of snake species. At the beginning of this century, scientists conducting general faunal surveys in the shrinking rainforests of the Uluguru Mountains of Tanzania failed to find the typhlopid snake *Letheobia uluguruensis* – a species known only from this locality. Indeed, no sightings of this species had been made in more than 70 years, so concern was expressed that this species might have gone extinct. However, in 2002 a different team 'rediscovered' *L. uluguruensis*, finding several specimens in soil in heavily disturbed habitat near to the forest edge. The rediscovery occurred probably because the 2002 team were especially looking for soil-dwelling amphibians and reptiles, and so had used the appropriate techniques (digging) needed to find this species.

LEFT New Guinea viper boa, *Candoia aspera*. The appearance of this small forest floor and semi-aquatic species is similar to the thick-set death adders, the Australo-Papuan elapid *Acanthophis*, and it may be a mimic of these venomous snakes.

Pacific boas

Four or five species of boa in the genus *Candoia* are unusual in that they occur in the area of New Guinea and nearby islands, almost as far away from other boas as is possible. Their dorsal body scales are strongly keeled, rather than only partially keeled or smooth as they are in most other boas, and they differ also in having a flat, angled rostral scale that gives the snout a distinctly oblique profile. *Candoia aspera* is a small, stout, semi-burrowing inhabitant of the forest floor, *C. carinata* is larger and slimmer and although mostly terrestrial is also found in trees, and *C. bibroni*, the largest and most slender, is almost exclusively arboreal.

Rosy and rubber boas

Two closely related and monotypic (containing only one species) genera from North America share burrowing habits and are relatively small, rarely growing over 1 m (3½ ft) long. The rubber boa, *Charina bottae*, is found further north than any other boa or python, even ranging into southwestern Canada. This species appears to be especially tolerant of cold. Active specimens have been measured with body temperatures of less than 7°C (44°F), although these snakes are unable to withstand the freezing temperatures of winter months and at this time hibernate underground. The rubber boa occurs in many habitats, from dry grasslands to humid woodlands and mountain forests, and may be found at altitudes above 3,000 m (9,800 ft). North America's other species, the rosy boa, *Lichanura trivirgata*, occurs in drier, desert areas of California and northwestern Mexico.

Rosy boas occasionally forage for food above ground, and rubber boas have even been known to climb trees to raid birds' nests, but they generally hunt and feed in underground tunnels. The feeding habits of the rubber boa are unusual, but are shared by the West African Calabar burrowing boa (see p.58). They capture and asphyxiate one or two small mice by trapping them with a coil of the body against the walls of their burrow while simultaneously swallowing another. At the same time

they use their short, stubby tail, the terminal vertebrae of which are fused into a bony club, to fend off attacks from the mother mouse. To divert her attention, the snake will even allow her to chew on its tail, so it is perhaps not surprising that the tails of rubber boas found in the wild are almost always heavily scarred.

Banana and Oaxacan boas

Two genera of small nocturnal boas live on the forest floors of Central America. *Ungaliophis* and *Exiliboa* were once thought to be closely related to the tropidophiids (dwarf boas, see p.70), and they do share several features of anatomy and behaviour, but are now thought to belong in the true boa family while dwarf boas are a distinct lineage. *Ungaliophis* contains two species with separate distributions in Central America, and the single species of *Exiliboa* (*E. placata*) is restricted to high-altitude cloud forests of Oaxaca, Mexico. The configuration of the head scales in these species is particularly distinctive. In *Ungaliophis*, the prefrontals are coalesced and expanded over much of the snout, whereas in *Exiliboa*, which has the more usual condition of paired prefrontals, it is the internasals that are fused, forming a single, large, triangular-shaped plate.

Occasional specimens of *Ungaliophis* reaching the USA in shipments of bananas led to them becoming commonly known as 'banana boas'. Their maxillary teeth are somewhat specialized and are perhaps modified for feeding on small, tree-dwelling frogs and lizards, their chief prey. The northern species, *U. continentalis*, lives mainly at low to intermediate altitudes from Chiapas, southern Mexico, to Honduras, though it is also known from above 2,000 m (6,600 ft) in the pine forests

of eastern Chiapas. *Ungaliophis panamensis*, the southern species, is found from southeastern Nicaragua through Costa Rica and Panama into northern Colombia. Adult *Ungaliophis* attain an overall length of about 70 cm (28 in). They are nocturnal and mainly arboreal.

The Oaxacan boa, *Exiliboa placata*, is found only in the cool, moist forests that prevail at 2,000–3,000 m (6,600–9,800 ft) on the mountain slopes of Oaxaca, Mexico. The generic name *Exiliboa* comes from the Latin 'exigere', 'to banish', in allusion to its isolated occurrence. A small snake, perhaps reaching no more than 50 cm (20 in), its body is compressed towards the base of the tail, where it is appreciably higher than wide, and external vestiges of limbs are present in both sexes. The dorsum is almost uniformly black. Specialized for burrowing in wet leaf litter, it preys mainly on small frogs and salamanders and their eggs.

Sand boas

There are 12 species of sand boas, which are sometimes grouped all together within the genus *Eryx*, although two or three of them are often placed in the genus *Gongylophis* and considered somewhat distinct. Small burrowers that occur over much of Asia and parts of northern Africa, they are particularly suited to life in sandy habitats: as listed on the next page.

RIGHT The European javelin, or spotted sand boa, *Eryx jaculus*.

BELOW RIGHT Rough-scaled sand boa, the South Asian *Gongylophis* (or *Eryx*) *conicus*.

- The skull is compact, and the small conical head has a rounded snout for burrowing into the sand head-first. In some species the lower jaw is also strongly countersunk.
- The body is cylindrical with a short tail.
- Many species have a hardened, horizontal ridge across the snout.
- The nostrils are on top of the snout, and in many species the openings have been reduced to narrow slits preventing earth and sand being drawn into the respiratory tract.
- Physiological adaptations enable them to reduce water loss and withstand the hot, dry conditions under which many live.

Like the rosy and rubber boas, most sand boas hunt for prey within subterranean tunnels, although some may also ambush prey by hiding in loose sand just beneath the surface, striking upwards at small animals that stumble over them. Most species eat small rodents and lizards, seizing them with a rapid, sidelong, slashing bite.

CONVERGENT EVOLUTION IN SNAKES

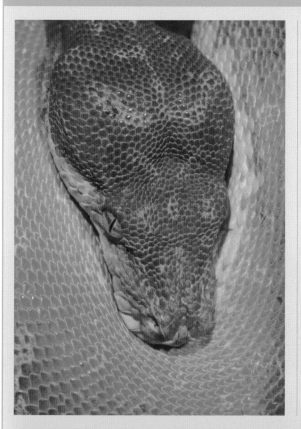

Some snakes living in different parts of the world bear a striking resemblance to each other, and, but for the often huge distances that separate them, one might easily assume they are closely related. The best-known example of this phenomenon is that of the green tree python, *Morelia viridis*, found in Australia and New Guinea, and the emerald tree boa, *Corallus caninus*, of South America.

These species are both tree-dwellers that change from yellow or brown as juveniles to bright green as adults. They are the same general size and shape, have similarly shaped heads with greatly enlarged anterior teeth, and also share the same style of resting in trees, looping their bodies over a horizontal branch. Even an expert may have to look twice to work out which is which. The reason why they are so similar, however, is not because they are especially closely related (they are classified in two different families), but because they have similar lifestyles and have both adapted to live in similar environments. Over the course of evolution they have been 'moulded' into similar-looking species by the same selective pressures.

ABOVE Green tree python, *Morelia viridis*.
BELOW Emerald tree boa, *Corallus caninus*.

BOLYERIIDAE AND XENOPHIIDAE:
Round Island 'Boas' and Spine-jawed Snakes

The 'boas' of Round Island (family Bolyeriidae) are of particular interest to biologists because of their uncertain origin and isolated distribution. Until recently, two species were known from this small landmass in the Indian Ocean, although owing to large-scale habitat destruction by goats and rabbits introduced in the nineteenth century, one (*Bolyeria multocarinata*) is probably now extinct. A single individual captured in the mid-1970s was the last to have been seen alive. Subfossil remains of a third, extinct species have been found on the nearby island of Mauritius.

Round Island boas were previously classified as a subfamily of the true boa family (Boidae). Unlike that of boids, however, the left lung is relatively much shorter (only about 10% or less of the length of the right lung), and there is no pelvis or vestiges of hindlimbs. In respect of these and certain other features Round Island 'boas' resemble

BELOW The Round Island boa, *Casarea dussumieri* is likely the only surviving species in its family, the Bolyeriidae.

LEFT Photograph taken in peninsular Malaysia of the only specimen of *Xenophidion schaeferi* ever found.

the 'higher snakes' (Caenophidia). Round Island boas are also unique among snakes in having the maxilla divided into movable front and rear parts.

Bolyeria multocarinata appears to have been a burrowing form, whereas the surviving species, *Casarea dussumieri*, is ground-dwelling and reaches a length of approximately 1.2 m (4 ft). Nocturnal in habit, it has been found by day hiding beneath fallen palm fronds, in the lower branches of trees, and in burrows excavated by nesting seabirds. It is oviparous, and feeds almost exclusively on the island's few endemic species of geckos and skinks. Although pushed to the brink of extinction, it is the target of conservation efforts, and its numbers are, it is to be hoped, increasing once more.

The family Xenophiidae comprises only two species in the genus *Xenophidion* (meaning 'strange snake'). Both were described as recently as 1995 (although they were discovered nearly 10 years prior to this) and each is known only from the original (holotype) specimen used to describe it. They have scale patterns and jaw anatomies that are quite divergent from any other known group, and researchers have struggled to interpret the family's relationship to other snake families. The results of a recent molecular study, however, suggest that they are most closely related to the Round Island boas and so they are mentioned in this section. The 'common' name, spine-jawed snakes, comes from a spiny projection that extends backwards from the upper jaw in both species. *Xenophidion acanthognathus* was collected in Borneo, and *X. schaeferi* was found in peninsular Malaysia, both in rainforest areas. Luckily the specimen of this latter species was found alive and photographed. Due to the scarcity of specimens and data, almost nothing is known of their natural history.

TROPIDOPHIIDAE: Dwarf 'Boas'

In certain features of anatomy, the two genera of small boa-like forms in the family Tropidophiidae resemble the larger, true boas of the family Boidae. With the exception of *Tropidophis semicinctus* they share the primitive feature of a pectoral girdle and, in males of most species, external vestiges of hindlimbs. Tropidophiids have a well-developed tracheal lung, and the left lung is greatly reduced or lacking altogether. Although snake biologists were not entirely surprised when DNA analyses began to indicate that tropidophiids were not especially closely related to true boas (and particularly the banana and Oaxacan boas, see p.64), many of them have been shocked at the latest results suggesting tropidophiids are most closely related to Neotropical pipe snakes (Aniliidae, see p.46). This will probably remain a matter of debate unless more supporting evidence can be found from morphology and additional DNA studies.

Neotropical in distribution, tropidophiids are small snakes with bodies that are cylindrical or slightly flattened from side to side, and most have relatively short, prehensile tails. Generally secretive and essentially nocturnal inhabitants of the forest floor, several *Tropidophis* are at least partially arboreal. Many are active foragers, feeding mainly on lizards and frogs, which they kill by constriction. The larger species of *Tropidophis* may occasionally also feed on small rodents and nestling birds. Except for *Trachyboa gularis*, all species are viviparous.

Prominent among the snakes of this family are just over 20 species of *Tropidophis*, most of which are distributed among the islands of the Caribbean, where the scarcity of other snakes and perhaps other favourable circumstances has permitted these forms to diversify and exploit a wide range of habitats. The genus is best represented on Cuba, with some 14 species found there. Three species survive as relics on the

RIGHT At slightly over 1 m (3/3 ft) long, the tropidophiid *Tropidophis melanurus*, from Cuba, is among the largest of the 'wood snakes' or 'dwarf boas'. This orange-coloured example is one of two main colour forms.

South American mainland, ranging from Ecuador (*T. battersbyi*) to Peru and Brazil (*T. paucisquamis* and *T. taczanowskyi*).

Most *Tropidophis* are dull brown or grey snakes with a variable pattern of dorsal body blotches and spots. Three Cuban species, *T. semicinctus*, *T. spiritus* and *T. wrighti*, are more conspicuously marked than most, with patterns of pale and dark bands or blotches. The scales on the dorsum are keeled in some species and smooth in others. Commonly also called 'wood snakes', *Tropidophis* occur predominantly in forested habitats, ranging from humid rainforest to dry *Acacia*–cactus scrub, and a relatively recently described Cuban species (*T. fuscus*) is known only from pine woods associated with red lateritic soils in the eastern part of the island. Most *Tropidophis* are terrestrial and typically found beneath logs, fallen palm fronds and other forest floor debris, and in ant and termite nests.

Tropidophis are unique among snakes for their extraordinary ability to autohaemorrhage, a form of behaviour that appears to have evolved as a defence reaction. If disturbed, their eyes turn red with blood, and the mouth begins to bleed freely from veins on the palate. Although alarming to observe, this does not seem to have any detrimental effect on the snake and, when danger has passed, it will quickly recover. It is not clear whether *Tropidophis* blood is actually an irritant (or poison) or whether the bleeding simply puts potential predators off. If molested, a *Tropidophis* may also coil up in a small ball with its head hidden in the centre, and produce an offensive-smelling anal secretion.

BELOW Spotted wood snake, the tropidophiid, *Tropidophis pardalis*.

Various other snakes (all of them North American colubrids) are reputed to adopt 'bleeding' behaviour. Long-nosed snakes (the colubrine *Rhinocheilus lecontei*) and eastern hognosed snakes (the dipsadine *Heterodon platyrhinos*) bleed from the cloaca, while the yellow-bellied water snake (the natricine *Nerodia erythrogaster*) sometimes exudes blood from the gums. In these species the bleeding may be incidental, caused by the wild thrashing they often resort to when molested, but in *Tropidophis* it appears to be more controlled and deliberate.

The other genus in the Tropidophiidae, *Trachyboa*, contains two small, stout-bodied species with an extremely short tail and strongly keeled scales. *Trachyboa boulengeri* has one or more enlarged, projecting scales over the eye and similar horn-like scales on the canthus (contour of the snout between the top and side of the head), a feature that has given rise to the name 'eyelash dwarf boa', by which both species are known. They feed almost exclusively on small frogs. *Trachyboa boulengeri* occurs in the humid lowland rainforests of Costa Rica, Panama, Ecuador and Colombia, while the other species, *T. gularis*, is found in the dry coastal forests of western Ecuador.

COLOUR CHANGE IN SNAKES

Several species of *Tropidophis*, and some other snakes, too, have the unusual ability to change colour, a curious phenomenon that appears to be associated with activity and generally follows a 24-hour cycle. Among the most striking is that demonstrated in *T. haetianus*, which, when active at night, has a pale yellow ground colour with two rows of dark dorsal markings, but during the day is almost completely black. *Tropidophis feicki* undergoes similar daily colour changes and should this species be subjected to a temperature of less than 17°C (63°F), it will adopt a transitional colour phase at any time of the day.

Colour change has also been reported in various other snakes, including *Boa constrictor*, Pacific boas (the boids *Candoia bibroni* and *C. carinata*), the Round Island 'boa' (the bolyeriid *Casarea dussumieri*), the western rattlesnake (the viperid *Crotalus viridis*) and most notably, the giant Oenpelli python, *Morelia oenpelliensis*, of northern Australia, which changes from a drab brown during the day to a ghostly silver-grey at night. A recently described homalopsid mud snake, *Enhydris gyii*, which when found was a deep brown with a red brown dorsum, was also observed changing colour and became almost white after being placed in a dark bucket. Darkening occurs when melanophores (pigment-containing cell structures) in the epidermis (outermost skin layer) move closer to the skin's surface; this is probably controlled by hormonal cues.

Colour change in individual snakes may also occur with development. Mussuranas (the dipsadine colubrid *Clelia clelia*) from Central and South America, for example, are bright red with a black head and pale neck collar as juveniles, whereas at about 60 cm (24 in) in length they change quite abruptly to uniform black or dark bluish-grey. Similarly, some arboreal, green species undergo a striking colour change with age. Young green tree pythons, *Morelia viridis*, from New Guinea and Australia, and emerald tree boas, *Corallus caninus*, from South America, for example, are yellow or orange-brown at first, while juveniles of the green colubrine colubrid *Boiga cyanea* from Southeast Asia are mainly brownish. Researchers do not fully understand why adults and juveniles of these particular snakes are so differently coloured, but it is probably mostly because different aged snakes are adapted to facing different environmental challenges.

Some snakes also undergo seasonal changes in colour, usually in response to reproductive cues or changes in their body condition. After they emerge from hibernation in spring, for example, the general ground colour of male European adders, *Vipera berus*, is a resplendent silver-grey, whereas after the reproductive season has finished they become drabber.

ACROCHORDIDAE: Asian/Australasian File Snakes

The Asian/Australasian file snakes, or 'wart snakes', of the family Acrochordidae are so called because of the coarse, granular appearance of their scales. Acrochordids are not to be confused with African 'file snakes', 13 or so species in the lamprophiine lamprophiid genus *Mehelya* (see p.114), that also have rough scales but not of a granular nature. Acrochordids form one of the most distinctive families of snakes, but comprise only one living genus (*Acrochordus*) with three species. In size and body proportions these unusual snakes resemble some pythons and boas, although in other features, such as a single lung, absence of a pelvis and hindlimbs, and aspects of the skull and jaw bones, they are more similar to many colubroid snakes. Recent analyses of DNA have confirmed results from morphological studies that indicate that acrochordids are the sister group to all other caenophidian snakes (Colubroidea), i.e. they form one half of the basal most split in the caenophidian evolutionary tree (see p.36).

Recent DNA studies have indicated that living acrochordids evolved over approximately the last 20 million years. The three living species occur from coastal India through the Thai-Malay peninsula and into New Guinea and northern Australia. Fossil acrochordids are known from deposits as old as 18 million years and are especially well known from localities in Pakistan and northern India. This is further inland and north and west than the distribution of the living species but they resemble them nonetheless in that they also lived in aquatic environments.

ABOVE The Arafura filesnake *Acrochordus arafurae*, an example from New Guinea. Note the granular scales, dorsally positioned eyes, and nostrils at the tip of the snout.

AQUATIC SPECIALISTS

Acrochordids are entirely aquatic. They occur mostly in estuarine and freshwater habitats, although the smallest acrochordid (*Acrochordus granulatus*, no more than about 1 m long) may also be found in coastal marine waters as far as 10 km (6¼ miles) offshore, often in areas frequented by true sea snakes. Much like sea snakes (see p.108), acrochordids have acquired a series of external and internal modifications that enable them to take full advantage of their aquatic surroundings. The only other major lineage of highly aquatic and at least partially marine snakes are the Asian mud snakes Homalopsidae (see p.90).

The most conspicuous feature of acrochordids is their skin, which is loose and baggy, and covered with small, tubercular (wart-like), non-overlapping scales. As a result, common names for *Acrochordus* in Malaysia and Indonesia include 'ular karung', 'ular kadut' and 'ular kain', which all mean sack or cloth snake. The largest species, *A. javanicus,* can exceed 2 m (6½ ft) in length and is also sometimes called 'elephant's trunk snake' in these countries. There are no broad, transverse scales on the abdomen, and the scales on the head are also all of the same general shape and form. Few other large snakes have such small, evenly sized scales on both the dorsal

RIGHT The aquatic Javan file snake, the acrochordid *Acrochordus javanicus*, hauled onto the bank for photographing. This species occurs from Thailand through to Java and Borneo, but acrochordids as a whole range in distribution from India through much of Indo-China and Southeast Asia to northern Australia and the southwest Pacific region.

and ventral surfaces of the body, and this particular quality has made the skin of *Acrochordus* prized in the leather trade. In Southeast Asia, many tens of thousands of specimens are probably harvested directly from the wild for this purpose every year (see p.16).

Acrochordids feed exclusively on fish. They may seize prey with a sudden sideways snap and subdue larger fish with the assistance of body loops. The coarse, 'gritty' nature of the scales may help restrain slippery, struggling prey. Observations of wild, free-ranging *A. arafurae* show that these snakes have very low feeding rates and may eat prey only a few times each year. Acrochordids are viviparous. Female *A. arafurae* produce litters of up to about 25 offspring, although this species reproduces less frequently than do most other snakes, perhaps as little as once every 10 years.

MALE OR FEMALE?

There are often few distinguishing external features between male and female snakes. Sexual dimorphism in these animals is typically limited externally to subtle differences in tail length and perhaps the relative numbers of scales on the abdomen (ventrals) and underside of the tail (subcaudals), although there are some snakes that differ more noticeably. Madagascan leaf-nosed snakes, the pseudoxyrhophiine lamprophiid *Langaha madagascariensis*, for example, have differently shaped appendages on the snout, while males and females of some sea snakes have different colour patterns.

In many snakes, females are larger than males, including natricines, pythons and especially anacondas. One of the more sexually dimorphic snakes studied to date is the Arafura acrochordid, *Acrochordus arafurae*. Females of this species are conspicuously larger and more heavy-bodied than males, have relatively larger heads and jaws, and have shorter tails. An adult female may attain a length of 2 m (6½ ft) and weigh more than 2 kg (4 lb 6 oz), whereas the much smaller males rarely exceed 1 m (3¼ ft) in length and average considerably less than 1 kg (2 lb 3 oz) in weight. Even when males and females are about the same length, the female's head is proportionally larger and its body much more heavy-set. These differences are apparent even in newborns.

Divergence in body size between the sexes of Arafura acrochordids has probably arisen through evolutionary selection for reproductive success – the larger the female's body, the larger her capacity for producing more offspring in a litter. The difference in relative head and jaw sizes, however, appears to be more the result of adaptations of males and females to different ecological niches rather than sexual selection – the sexes have undergone independent specialization over time to take advantage of different food resources and thereby increase their success rates in hunting. Females have been shown to hunt in deeper water than males and generally eat only a single large fish, whereas males tend to inhabit shallower water and eat a larger number of smaller fish. As adults, the sexes also feed on different species of fish.

LOW METABOLISM AND OTHER CURIOUS FEATURES

Acrochordids have an unusually low rate of metabolism (only about half that of other snakes) and appear incapable of sustained activity for more than a few minutes. Their low metabolic rates are also associated with low reproductive rates. There are differences among the three species, but *A. arafurae* females might reproduce only once every few years. Out of the water they are generally sluggish and seem almost helpless. Studies of *Acrochordus arafurae*, however, have shown that these snakes, although slow in their movements, are capable of travelling for considerable distances in the seasonally flooded billabongs of northern Australia where they occur. During the day they remain hidden under overhanging banks, beneath sunken logs, or amongst waterweed, but while searching for food at night they frequently cover distances of several hundred metres.

In addition to their remarkably low metabolism, acrochordids are highly unusual in other regards. They have tiny hair-like projections on their scales, particularly dense on the head, that sense movement in the often murky water they live in. *Acrochordus granulatus* have very high volumes of blood for their size, and their blood also carries a higher concentration of red blood cells than in other snakes. These features combine to allow them to hold a large amount of oxygen, preventing the need to come to the water surface frequently to breathe.

XENODERMATIDAE: Strange-skinned Snakes

The family Xenodermatidae comprises a very poorly understood, fairly small lineage of snakes. They are relatively little studied, and there is great uncertainty as to which snakes should actually be classified within this family. Some workers have argued that, based on morphological features such as patterns of reduced head scalation and peculiar nostrils, this is a much larger and more widespread family than generally believed, but most snake biologists currently consider the family restricted

BELOW An example of the xenodermatid *Xenodermus javanicus*, found at night on the edge of a small rocky stream in a rainforest in Java.

to about four genera and 15 species from Southeast Asia. There is evidence from DNA that these at least comprise a single distinct lineage, but until more snakes are studied for their DNA the true limits of this group remain somewhat uncertain. The 15 or so Southeast Asian species are rather peculiar-looking snakes with long bodies, distinctively enlarged heads, long tails, and, in some species, oddly formed scales. Among the more widely distributed and best known is *Xenodermus javanicus*, from Thailand, Malaysia, Java and Sumatra. This unusual little snake, only about 70 cm (28 in) long, has grain-shaped dorsal scales, with three rows of large, keeled tubercles. On its lower sides the scales are triangular and separated by areas of bare skin – which gives the snake its name, with 'xeno' meaning strange and 'dermis' skin. A frog-eater, it lives in wet leaf litter or waterlogged soil in tropical forests, swamps, marshes and rice paddies, where for much of the time it leads a semi-aquatic or partly burrowing existence. *Xenodermus* has most often been encountered by biologists who conduct fieldwork at night, when it can be found actively foraging on the surface. The other members of the Xenodermatidae occur in Borneo and into Indochina, Japan and northeast India.

PAREATIDAE: Slug Snakes

There are currently 14 species of snake recognized in the family Pareatidae, classified in the genera *Aplopeltura*, *Asthenodipsas* and *Pareas*. They are found throughout East and South Asia and subsist largely on terrestrial gastropod molluscs, giving rise to the common name snail or slug snakes. The dietary specialization of pareatids is shared with several Neotropical snakes in the Dipsadinae subfamily of Colubridae (species of *Dipsas*, *Sibon* and *Sibynomorphus*) and, despite their different evolutionary origins, they resemble each other closely in appearance. Most snail-eating snakes are small – less than 1 m (3¼ ft) in length. The head is often large, with protruding eyes, and the snout is usually short and blunt. They are adapted for climbing, with long bodies flattened from side to side, and the head well differentiated from the slender neck.

These snakes eat only the soft body of the snail inside the shell; grasping the body with its needle-like teeth, the snake extends its jaws alternately from side to side and continues advancing its grip in this way until the mollusc is dragged bodily from its shell. Interestingly, some snail-eating pareatids have been found to have asymmetrical jaws, with more teeth on the right lower jaw than on the left. This is thought to aid them while foraging, because the vast majority of snails display dextral (clockwise) whorls. In experiments where the Japanese *Pareas iwasakii* were fed artificially bred sinistral (anti-clockwise) and dextral prey, they were able to extract the body of dextral snails from their shells faster than sinistral ones, and dropped the sinistral snails more often. Some snail-eating aquatic arthropods also have asymmetrical feeding apparatus. Two species of snail-eaters from Africa (of the pseudoxyrhophiine lamprophiid genus *Duberria*) occasionally deal with larger snails by smashing their shells on the ground, as some birds do, but these species are not closely related to the Asian pareatid or New World dipsadine snail/slug eaters.

LEFT Malayan slug-eating snake, the pareatid *Pareas vertebralis*. Slug and snail-eating snakes are generally small, secretive creatures and most are nocturnal. They locate prey by following the trails of mucus that slugs and snails leave behind as they move about.

VIPERIDAE: Vipers

Vipers comprise the family Viperidae, and these are nearly 300 species of highly specialized snakes with a characteristic venom-injecting apparatus that is more sophisticated than that found in any other group. Unlike mambas, coral snakes and other elapids, vipers have large, erectile fangs that are capable of being 'pivoted' independently of one another (see p.13). Normally, these are kept folded back along the roof of the mouth, encased in a protective sheath of soft tissue (the vagina dentis), but are rotated forwards as the mouth is opened to strike. The fangs have enclosed venom canals and their large size enables vipers to inject venom deep into the tissues of their prey, where it is rapidly absorbed; in this respect the fangs can be compared with a hypodermic needle. A West African species, the Gabon viper, *Bitis gabonica*, is credited with having the longest fangs of all, measuring around 5 cm (2 in). Only the stiletto snakes (atractaspidine lamprophiids of the genus *Atractaspis*, see p.111) have similarly large, front-mounted, hollow and movable fangs, but in this group

the articulation between the maxilla and the rest of the skull is uniquely developed into a ball-and-socket joint.

Vipers are usually characterized as heavy-bodied, terrestrial snakes, and adaptive radiation in this family has perhaps not been as extensive as in some others. With the exception of a few desert-dwelling forms that, by shuffling their bodies are able to 'sink' vertically into loose sand, none are habitual burrowers, and only one North American species, the cottonmouth, *Agkistrodon piscivorus*, is semi-aquatic. There are though, many tree-dwelling species that have relatively slender bodies with strongly prehensile tails.

The Viperidae has an almost worldwide distribution and embraces three subfamilies: the night adders plus 'true' vipers (Viperinae); the Azemiopinae, with a single species; and the pit vipers (Crotalinae). A Eurasian species, the common viper or adder (the viperine *Vipera berus*), has a particularly large range, including areas within the Arctic Circle, further north than any other snake. The snake with a range that extends further south than any other species is also a viper, the Patagonian lancehead (the crotaline *Rhinocerophis ammodytoides*).

FEEDING HABITS OF VIPERS

Vipers are among the greatest exponents of the 'sit-and-wait' hunting technique, and many have evolved highly cryptic body markings that enable them to remain concealed from their predators and the animals on which they feed. Using chemical traces of their prey to seek out strategic ambush sites, they lie in wait for a meal to pass within striking reach, remaining motionless in the same place often for days or even weeks until either their patience is finally rewarded or instinct drives them to try elsewhere.

In some vipers the tip of the tail is coloured differently and used as a lure for attracting prey. Peringuey's adders (the viperine *Bitis peringueyi*) buried in desert sand, will wriggle their black-and-white-banded tail tips above the surface to attract foraging lizards, and the spider-tailed viper (see p.84) is even more remarkable. Similar luring behaviour is seen in some non-viperid snakes, such as the death adders (*Acanthophis*, Family Elapidae) from Australia and New Guinea.

The bite of a viper takes the form of a rapid 'stabbing' movement, for which the fangs are fully erected and the mouth opened to almost 180˚ (see p.13). If the prey is small, the snake may restrain it in its mouth until the venom takes effect, but in many cases it withdraws its fangs immediately, and locates the dying animal afterwards by following its scent. Throughout the snake's life the fangs are continuously replaced by others that grow and move forward from behind; when the next-in-line is ready for use, the functioning fang loosens at its base and either falls out or is left embedded in the body of the snake's next meal. The venom of many vipers has a pronounced digestive effect on their prey, and this is believed to be a major contributory factor in the ability of some species to live in seasonally cold environments, where low temperatures may otherwise restrict effective digestion.

OPPOSITE With a scaly horn on the tip of its snout, the nose-horned viper, *Vipera ammodytes*, from the eastern Mediterranean region is one of the more distinctive European/western Asian vipers.

RIGHT Rhombic night adder, the viperine viperid *Causus rhombeatus*. Night adders are African terrestrial snakes that feed largely on amphibians, especially toads.

SUBFAMILY VIPERINAE: Night Adders and 'True' Vipers
Night adders

Six species of night adder, all within the single genus *Causus*, are found only in Africa, south of the Sahara Desert. Although night adders generally live up to their name, some species have been seen venturing out in broad daylight or basking in the morning and evening. The most widespread species is the rhombic night adder, *C. rhombeatus*, which occurs throughout the larger part of the continent. They have smooth scales, symmetrically arranged on the crown of the head, and eyes with round pupils, and thus differ from most other vipers in overall appearance. Night adders are also in the minority among vipers in laying eggs as opposed to giving birth. Typically less than 80 cm (32 in) long, most are brown or grey with patterns of spots or blotches.

BELOW Velvety night adder, the viperine viperid *Causus resimus*, from Africa.

The snout of an East African species (*C. defilippi*) is upturned and perhaps used for rooting out its prey. Although comparatively inoffensive, when thoroughly aroused night adders draw the body into a defensive coil, inflate themselves with air, and emit a surprisingly loud, guttural hiss. Night adders have large venom glands. Their venom is especially toxic to toads, their natural prey, but appears to be rather less dangerous to humans than that of other vipers.

WHICH SNAKE IS THE MOST DANGEROUS?

LEFT Asian saw-scaled viper, the viperine *Echis carinatus*.

The frequently asked question 'which snake in the world has the most lethal venom?' is difficult to answer decisively because much depends on the method of testing. However, the inland taipan or fierce snake, *Oxyuranus microlepidotus*, an Australian relative of the cobras, is perhaps more venomous than any other snake – a single bite delivers enough to kill more than 200,000 mice, or at least 12 adult humans. The eastern brown snake (the Australian elapid *Pseudonaja textilis*) is among the closest challengers. Whether or not the inland taipan is the most dangerous in terms of the everyday lives of humans, however, is a different matter. Inland taipans are shy and rarely encountered snakes found only in the remote outback of western Queensland, where few people have ever even seen one.

The group of species responsible for the greatest number of fatal accidents, and thus overall probably the most dangerous of all venomous snakes, are the saw-scaled or carpet vipers (*Echis*). These widely distributed snakes are found throughout much of northern Africa, the Middle East, India and Asia, often in close proximity to human habitation, and in places they may be remarkably abundant. Owing to their small size and highly cryptic colour pattern, they are difficult to detect and may easily be stepped on. They also have very potent venom, and their potentially dangerous nature is further enhanced by the fact that they can strike out with little provocation. Among various other potentially dangerous species, responsible for a large proportion of snakebite fatalities in humans, are the Neotropical lancehead pit vipers (species of the genera

Bothrops, Bothrocophias, Bothriopsis, Bothropoides and *Rhinocerophis*) from Central and South America; the puff adder (the viperid *Bitis arietans*) and mambas (the elapid *Dendroaspis*) of Africa; the cobras (the elapid *Naja*) of Africa, India and Southeast Asia; Russell's viper (*Daboia russellii*) of India and *D. siamensis* of Southeast Asia; and the elapids in the New Guinea and Australian region: death adders (*Acanthophis*), the common taipan (*Oxyuranus scutellatus*), the tiger snake (*Notechis scutatus*) and brown snakes (*Pseudonaja*).

Bites from venomous snakes are a major health risk in some parts of the world, and on average are believed to cause the death of more than 100,000 people each year. They can be a threat to the safety and livelihoods of humans, especially those living in rural areas where snakes are more likely to be encountered and medical help in the event of an accident may be many hours or even days away. It would be wrong to assume, however, that the bite of a dangerously venomous snake has only one inevitable outcome. The percentage of deaths reported each year in relation to the number of people bitten is actually very small; one need only look at the details of a few case histories to appreciate that the symptoms and severity of snakebite depend on a wide range of circumstances. These include the size and age of the snake in question, quantity of venom injected, individual sensitivity of the victim, level of medical care and time taken to reach hospital, to name only a few. Even if one is unfortunate enough to be bitten by a venomous snake, this does not necessarily always lead to the injection of venom and the development of symptoms. Venom is a precious commodity that requires energy and time to produce and, as their principal means of obtaining food, most snakes will not expend it needlessly when defending themselves. Based on studies of proven bites by particular species, the ratio of bites to envenomation is usually about 2:1. It should also be remembered that, although potentially dangerous, many venomous snakes are extremely beneficial to humans by controlling pest species such as rodents.

True vipers

The 'true' vipers, of which there are over 80 species divided among 13 genera, are restricted to the Old World regions of Europe, Asia and Africa. They differ most conspicuously from pit vipers (Crotalinae) in lacking facial heat-sensitive pits. The subfamily Viperinae used to include only the true vipers and exclude the night adders, *Causus*, which were confined to a separate subfamily (Causinae). However, the latest research shows that true vipers might not comprise a natural grouping because some are possibly more closely related to night adders than to other true vipers. The details have yet to be worked out and true vipers are discussed here together as an informal group of broadly similar appearance and biology.

Just over 20 species of the genus *Vipera* occur mostly in Europe and parts of Asia, where in places (such as Britain) they are the only venomous snakes. They are all fairly heavy-bodied snakes with short tails, well-defined, triangular heads, relatively large head scales, and a distinctive zigzag pattern along the body. Some species, such as the nose-horned viper, *V. ammodytes*, have a scaly 'nose-horn' on the tip of the snout. Terrestrial, they occur in a variety of habitats including open forests, sandy heaths, wet meadows, and dry, rocky hillsides.

Two particularly widespread species, the European viper or adder, *V. berus*, and asp viper, *V. aspis*, are found at altitudes of up to about 3,000 m (9,800 ft) in the European Alps. All species are active by day, although at least some become partly nocturnal when night-time temperatures are high enough. Most hibernate during winter, often in communal dens, and after emerging in spring some migrate short distances to different feeding grounds. While most feed on rodents and lizards, the small meadow viper, *V. ursinii*, eats mainly insects. Four similar species in the northern African and southern Asian genus *Macrovipera* and two in the widespread Asian genus *Daboia* are larger snakes characterized by small head scales.

BELOW The adder, the viperine viperid *Vipera berus*, is one of the world's most successful snakes. It has the largest geographical distribution of any terrestrial land-living species, ranging from the British Isles, across Europe and northern Asia, east to the Pacific Ocean, and also occurs further north than any other snake. Adders exhibit considerable colour dimorphism; top, year-old juvenile; bottom left, reproductively active male; bottom right, female.

Among the most dangerous of all snakes are the nine or so species of saw-scaled or carpet vipers (*Echis*) from North Africa, the Middle East and Asia, which are responsible for several thousand snakebite fatalities each year. When alarmed, these irascible little snakes rub the coils of their bodies together, producing a curious rasping sound that serves to warn off many potential predators without the snake having to resort to wasting venom.

The 14 species of African bush vipers (*Atheris*) are distinctive-looking snakes with short, rounded heads and large eyes. Some are brightly coloured and have peculiarly fringed scales. Found in the equatorial forests of Africa, most are tree-dwellers. Two related species, Hindi's viper, *Montatheris hindii*, from high-altitude moorlands in Kenya, and the lowland swamp viper, *Proatheris superciliaris*, from Mozambique, Malawi and Tanzania, are ground-dwelling.

Some 16 or so species in the exclusively African/Arabian genus *Bitis* are exceptionally stout-bodied vipers with broad, flattened, triangular heads. All are strictly ground-dwelling. With a distribution extending throughout Africa and into southern Arabia, the puff adder, *B. arietans*, is the most common and widespread, while the massively built Gaboon viper, *B. gabonica*, is the largest, attaining lengths of almost 2 m (6½ ft) and weights of over 10 kg (22 lb). This formidable snake has been known to eat small antelopes and even porcupines. Gaboon vipers and a similar-looking species, the river jack, *B. nasicornis*, are tropical-forest-dwellers with curious scaly horns on the tip of the snout and camouflaging colour patterns that resemble dead leaves.

ABOVE Although not a pit viper, the facial nerve endings in Russell's viper, the Asian viperine *Daboia russelli*, are highly sensitive to temperature variation. Several other snakes that lack externally visible pits also have heat-sensitive areas on their heads, including puff adders, *Bitis arietans*, and *Boa constrictor*.

LEFT Great Lakes bush viper, *Atheris nitschei*, an East African viperine often found in the peripheral forests around Lake Victoria and other large lakes. The milky-coloured eyes are a symptom of the skin-shedding process.

RIGHT Horned sand viper, *Cerastes cerastes*. This northern African and Arabian desert viperine buries itself in sand where it lies in wait for prey with only its eyes and nostrils visible.

BELOW RIGHT The Iranian spider-tailed viperine viperid, *Pseudocerastes urarachnoides*, in ambush posture.

Other species, such as the horned adder, *B. caudalis*, are small desert-dwellers with conspicuous horn-like projections over the eyes, a feature they share with seven species of African and Asian sand vipers (*Cerastes* and *Pseudocerastes*). The latter had an interesting addition in 2006 with the description of the spider-tailed viper, *P. urarachnoides*. Found in Iran, this species has extremely elongated scales on the tip of its tail, which ends in a bulbous growth. The feature bears a strong resemblance to a spider, or more precisely a 'sun spider' (Order Solifugae – not true spiders), which live in the same habitat. It has been speculated that the snake uses this ornament as a lure for prey and it even moves the tail in a jerky, arachnid-esque manner, which adds to the ruse.

Macmahon's viper, *Eristicophis macmahoni*, a similarly unusual species from western Pakistan, has peculiar, whorl-like rows of heavily keeled scales, with a shovel-shaped rostral scale. Many of these desert vipers have developed a unique sidewinding method of progression to overcome the difficulties of moving across loose, shifting sand (see p.19).

SUBFAMILY AZEMIOPINAE: Fea's Viper

Fea's viper, *Azemiops feae*, is the only representative of the subfamily Azemiopinae. It is a rarely encountered species found only in the remote and wet mountain cloud forests of southern and central China, northern Burma (Myanmar), Tibet, and Vietnam. It is quite a small viper, measuring up to perhaps 1 m (3¼ ft), and it retains some relatively primitive features for vipers, so its lineage was previously thought to form one half of the first branching in the viper evolutionary tree. For example, *Azemiops* superficially resembles elapid or 'colubrid' snakes in that the top of its head is covered with large symmetrical plates instead of an array of smaller and more numerous scales. However, the latest DNA analyses demonstrate that viperines are more closely related to *Azemiops* than to crotalines. The body scales of *Azemiops* are all smooth, a feature it shares with only one other species of viper, *Calloselasma rhodostoma*, a pit viper from Southeast Asia. Little is known about the natural history of *Azemiops*, other than that it is a ground-dwelling, oviparous snake that lays clutches of about five eggs. Nocturnal or crepuscular, it feeds on shrews and small rodents. Like pit vipers, it may vibrate its tail and gape when threatened, although its venom yields are very small and so it is not considered a threat to humans.

BELOW The Indochinese Fea's viper, *Azemiops feae*, is the only representative of the viperid subfamily Azemiopinae.

SUBFAMILY CROTALINAE: Rattlesnakes and Other Pit Vipers

Species in this subfamily include the rattlesnakes (*Crotalus*) and about 26 other genera distributed throughout the Americas and South and Southeast Asia. Their most characteristic feature is a pair of heat-sensitive pit organs on each side of the head used for locating prey. All pythons and at least some boas of the genera *Corallus*, *Epicrates* and *Boa* also have heat-sensitive pits, but these occur on, between or behind the scales of the lips (labials), while the crotaline vipers have a single large pit on each side of the face between the eye and nostril. The pit organs of the pit vipers are more sophisticated in that they consist of two compartments, divided in the middle by a membranous diaphragm. The smaller, inner part is connected by a narrow duct to a small pore in front of the eye, which appears to be a means of balancing the air pressure on either side of the diaphragm, and also measures the ambient air temperature. The larger outer chamber opens as a wide, forwardly directed aperture, through which infrared radiation emitted by prey enters and is detected by a series of highly sensitive thermoreceptive cells.

The heat-sensitive pits of snakes are extraordinarily sensitive to temperature variation, and experiments have shown that those of some pit vipers can detect changes in temperature of as little as 0.001°C (0.002°F). This renders the organs of use in hunting even 'cold-blooded' prey such as frogs, which are often just a little warmer than the surrounding environment. Using these organs, the snake can locate prey, or predators, even in complete darkness. A pit viper deprived of its senses of sight and smell, for example, can perceive a mouse 10°C (18°F) warmer than its surroundings from a distance of 70 cm (28 in), and guide the direction of its strike accordingly to within about 5°.

ABOVE The heat-sensory pit in this cascabel or Neotropical rattlesnake, the crotaline viperid *Crotalus durissus*, can be seen clearly as a dark hole in the side of the face.

RIGHT The jumping pit viper *Atropoides* is a Neotropical crotaline viperid genus. This species, *A. nummifer*, from Central America is typical in having a stout body that is almost triangular in cross section.

Rattlesnakes, of which there are about 35 species, mostly in the genus *Crotalus*, are inhabitants of dry woodlands, prairies and rocky desert environments, mainly in North America and Mexico. One species, the cascabel, *C. durissus*, ranges through southern Central America into South America. They are all rather stout-bodied snakes that range in length from the two 60 cm (24 in) long pygmy rattlesnakes (in the genus *Sistrurus*) to the big eastern diamondback, *C. adamanteus*, which may exceed 2 m (6½ ft). In newborn snakes the characteristic tail rattle, from which these pit vipers take their name, is at first only a small button. Additional segments accumulate with successive moults of the skin, and when the rattle becomes too large, the last and oldest segments break off. The rattle is used only for defence and at least one species, the Santa Catalina Island rattlesnake, *C. catalinensis*, has lost it during evolution; perhaps because it has no natural predators there is little need for such an adaptation, and, because it hunts arboreal prey, there is potentially a greater need for stealth.

THE VIPERS OF QUEIMADA GRANDE

LEFT Golden lancehead, the crotaline viperid *Bothropoides insularis*.

A small, deserted island off the eastern coast of Brazil barely 1 km (³⁄₅ mile) across at its widest point, Queimada Grande is a refuge for large numbers of birds. It is renowned mostly, however, for its other main inhabitant, an endemic species of pit viper that occurs in extraordinary abundance. The golden lancehead, *Bothropoides insularis*, is a slender and unusually pale-coloured species that probably diverged from its larger mainland relative, the jararaca, *Bothropoides jararaca*, when the island was separated from the Brazilian coast about 11,000 years ago. It subsists almost entirely on the various species of small birds that use the island as a reviving 'stop-off' point while on migration, and relies on its potent, fast-acting venom to kill prey before they have a chance to fly away.

Walking through the island's wooded interior, it is not unusual to spot a golden lancehead every few paces. Commonly seen in trees, they may also be encountered among leaves on the ground, nestled between tree roots, on rock faces, and in almost every other accessible habitat. That so many of these snakes should occur in an area so small seems remarkable. There are, however, no other kinds of venomous snakes on Queimada Grande with which the lancehead might otherwise need to compete for food and shelter, and neither does it have any significant predators. With a more or less regular supply of birds, its principal food source is also almost always available.

Golden lanceheads are undoubtedly potentially dangerous snakes but, contrary to popular belief, their venom is in fact less lethal than that of many mainland *Bothropoides* species, including their presumed nearest relative, *B. jararaca*, at least as assessed by mouse LD_{50} tests (see p.23). The erroneous reputation of high lethality in the venom of this species appears to have originated from some late-nineteenth-century experiments with unreported methods. There have been several repeated experiments in recent years in which the reported high lethality of *B. insularis* venom has not been replicated. It would be interesting to know whether the venom of this species is relatively more lethal to birds, its natural prey.

Some other pit vipers are similarly successful on other islands elsewhere, feeding on birds and attaining very high densities, notably *Gloydius shedaoensis* on Shedao off the northeastern coast of China.

RIGHT AND BELOW Caterpillar of *Hemeroplanes triptolemus* mimicking a Neotropical palm (or eyelash) pit viper, *Bothriechis schlegelii* (below). If molested, the caterpillar will even behave in the same defensive manner as a viper, reacting with quick, sideways-directed 'strikes'.

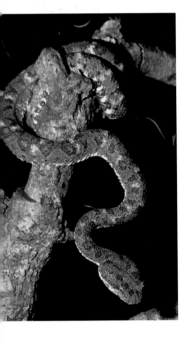

None of the remaining pit viper genera has a rattle, although many will vibrate their tails among dry leaves when alarmed, which has the effect of creating a similar sound. Among the most diverse of the Latin American forms are the more than 40 species of fer-de-lance (*Bothrops* and related genera), named after their characteristic lance-shaped heads. All are highly venomous, and they include such notorious species as the terciopelo, *Bothrops asper*, from Mexico and Central America, and the South American jararaca, *Bothropoides jararaca*, and urutu, *Rhinocerophis alternatus*. So feared is the bite of the South American bushmaster, *Lachesis muta*, the world's largest viper at up to about 3 m (10 ft), that in parts of its range it has been given the name matabuey, meaning 'ox-killer'. Bushmasters have rather peculiar knob-like scales and they share this feature with Central and northern South American jumping vipers (*Atropoides*), a group of six exceptionally stout-bodied snakes named for their ability to strike with such force that the body is often carried forward with the momentum. Other ground-dwelling pit vipers from the Americas include four species of the genus *Agkistrodon*, of which the copperhead, *A. contortrix*, is an abundant species found over much of the eastern USA, and the cottonmouth, *A. piscivorous*, is unique among vipers in being semi-aquatic. Eight hognosed pit vipers (*Porthidium*) are inhabitants mostly of Neotropical lowland tropical forests, while two species of Mexican horned vipers (*Ophryacus*) and four of montane pit vipers (*Cerrophidion*) live high in the mountains of southern Mexico and Central America. Nine species of palm vipers (*Bothriechis*) are Neotropical climbers, characterized by slender bodies, strongly prehensile tails, and beautifully mottled green colour patterns that are perhaps unsurpassed in concealing these snakes among leafy trees.

Many Old World pit vipers were historically grouped in the ecologically diverse genus *Trimeresurus*. Now subdivided into at least 11 different genera, these snakes occur throughout much of Asia including numerous islands in the western Pacific Ocean. The Asian pit vipers are morphologically fairly conservative. Many are tree-climbers and some, such as Pope's pit viper, *Popeia popeiorum*, the white-lipped pit viper, *Cryptelytrops albolabris*, and most members of the genus *Viridovipera*, display a similar and characteristic leaf-green colour pattern. Five similar Southeast Asian species now in the genus *Tropidolaemus* are distinguished from other forms by keeled chin scales, and include the strikingly marked temple viper, *T. wagleri*. Other snakes previously classified in *Trimeresurus* include various ground-dwelling pit vipers known from Asia. Five very thick-bodied species of *Ovophis* include the mountain pit viper,

ABOVE Indochinese white-lipped pit viper, *Cryptelytrops albolabris*.

BELOW Greatest of the pit vipers and largest of all venomous snakes in the western hemisphere, the bushmaster may reach an adult size of more than 3.5 m (11½ ft). Four species are recognized, of which this example, from Ecuador, is the common form, *Lachesis muta*.

O. monticola, a species found throughout much of Asia, from India to China and Taiwan. One particularly large species, the Okinawa habu, *Protobothrops flavoviridis*, of Japan, may attain lengths of 2.2 m (7 ft).

Other Old World pit vipers include three or four species of hump-nosed vipers (*Hypnale*) from southwestern India and Sri Lanka and the Chinese sharp-nosed viper, *Deinagkistrodon acutus*, from southeastern China and Taiwan. These are tropical forest forms characterized by upturned snouts. Some 12 species of *Gloydius* are small inhabitants of temperate forests and mountains in western and southern Asia. One of these, *G. himalayanus*, occurs at altitudes of up to 4,900 m (16,000 ft) in the Himalayas. Among the Asian pit vipers is the Malayan, *Calloselasma rhodostoma*, a species that is widespread in Southeast Asia and the cause of many snakebite accidents in this region. In common with a number of other Asian pit vipers, and unlike most of its New World relatives, it is an egg-layer.

ABOVE Malayan pit viper, *Calloselasma rhodostoma*. This potentially dangerously venomous crotaline viperid is found throughout much of Southeast Asia, but despite its common name it occurs in only a small part of peninsular Malaysia.

HOMALOPSIDAE: Mud Snakes
(tentacled snakes, mangrove snakes and other Old World aquatics)

A highly aquatic family of snakes, members of the Homalopsidae tend to inhabit slow-moving or stagnant water, which gives rise to one of their common names, the mud snakes. From Southeast Asia and coastal northern Australia, they are found in both freshwater and coastal environments and have various specializations for aquatic life, such as nostrils set on the end of the snout that can be closed by valves when submerging, and small, upwardly facing eyes. There are currently 10 genera and approximately 40 species of homalopsids, which are all rear-fanged and not regarded as dangerously venomous to humans. Most are smallish snakes with relatively thick-set bodies, the stoutest being Bocourt's homalopsid, *Enhydris bocourti*, from West Malaysia, Cambodia, Thailand and Vietnam, and the longest probably being *Homalopsis buccata*, one female of which was found measuring 1.37 m (4½ ft). Another Southeast Asian species of river mouths and coastal waters, the keel-bellied homalopsid, *Bitia hydroides*, has features more typically associated with some true (elapid) sea snakes, such as reduced ventral scales, and a tail flattened from side to side. Juvenile specimens even display a small head and neck widening to a large body, as seen in several true sea snakes.

Homalopsids feed mostly on fish and tend to eat a greater number of smaller prey items than most snakes, often consuming several in one feeding session, which they capture by ambush or by feeling around for them in muddy water. The tentacled snake, *Erpeton tentaculatum*, has long, paired protuberances on the end of its snout that have a sensory function, helping it detect prey by touch. These tentacles are a few millimetres in length and extremely rich in nerve endings, enabling the snake to detect the slightest movement in the water, a feature that is particularly useful when foraging in murky environments. These completely aquatic snakes live in slow-moving streams and when hunting wait in a characteristic 'J' shape, with the bend between their body and head. Sometimes anchored by their tails to submerged twigs or plants, they hang in the current and strike to seize passing fish. Other homalopsids also use this technique, but the tentacled snake enhances its chance of catching a meal by exploiting its prey's escape reflex when hunting. When fish are disturbed they quickly move to the right or left in milliseconds. The tentacled snake exploits this by first startling passing fish with a subtle movement that runs down the length of its body, and then striking accurately as the fish respond.

From Australia and New Guinea, three species of bockadams (*Cerberus*) are nocturnal snakes that inhabit estuaries and hunt mainly for mudskippers on mudflats exposed at low tide. Other mangrove-dwelling homalopsid species in the Indo-Pacific feed on crustaceans, including Gerard's homalopsid, *Gerarda prevostiana*, which eats freshly moulted mangrove crabs. This species has been observed wrapping its body around a crab and using its mouth to tear off manageable chunks. It is one of the only snakes known to break up its food before it eats. Another estuarine species found over much of the Australo-Papuan region and also in Southeast Asia, the white-bellied mangrove snake, *Fordonia leucobalia*, also feeds exclusively on crustaceans, and is armed with robust fangs for piercing their exoskeletons. It eats mud lobsters and mangrove crabs in the intermoult (hard-shelled) stage and has been known to pull the legs off crabs that are otherwise too large to consume.

ABOVE View from above of the head of *Erpeton tentaculatum*, showing the sensory 'tentacles'.

LEFT The homalopsid, *Enhydris plumbea*.

It seems that all homalopsids are viviparous, although little is known about the reproductive ecology of several species. The nourishment of embryos via a placenta has been studied in some members of the family. Female homalopsids are known to continue feeding while gravid, unlike most snakes, which may reflect their ability to continue supplying nutrients to the embryos after impregnation, as well as the group's diet of numerous, small prey items.

Paradoxically, crabs pose a considerable threat to some small homalopsid snakes, which they are known to eat, as do large predatory fish and other snake species, including elapids such as the Indian cobra, *Naja naja*, and the banded krait, *Bungarus fasciatus*. For the rainbow mud snake, *Enhydris enhydris*, common throughout Southeast Asia in large lakes disturbed by human activity, its biggest threat is human exploitation.

This species makes up about 70% of the catch in what is considered the world's largest snake-hunting operation. Every year at Tonlé Sap (the Great Lake) in Cambodia nearly 7 million snakes of 11 different species are caught by local fishermen. Six of these species are homalopsids and they are used primarily as feed in the growing crocodile farm industry, although about half the *Homalopsis buccata* caught are sold for their skin, as are a considerable number of *Enhydris boccourti*. As stocks of fish have been depleted in the lake, snakes offer a tempting alternative for use as human and animal feed and, since it was first documented in the late 1990s, the number of fishermen turning their attention to snakes has increased dramatically. The sustainability of this practice or its long-term affects on the local snake populations are difficult to measure, but data collected between 2000 and 2005 show that catch per unit effort has declined by about 80%, which might indicate a substantial fall in numbers. Interestingly, *H. buccata* and *E. boccourti* populations seem to show the greatest declines despite the overall catches for these species being quite low, which might be because these species produce relatively few offspring and because larger individuals are targeted for use in the skin trade, removing the most fecund females from populations.

ELAPIDAE: Cobras, Coral Snakes, Kraits, Taipans and Sea Snakes

The Elapidae is a diverse family of venomous snakes, and includes some of the largest and most formidable species known. Various elapids, such as the coral snakes, kraits and some sea snakes, are also among the most spectacularly coloured. As a group, the approximately 60 genera and 350 or so species are characterized by enlarged, non-erectile fangs in the front of the mouth (see p.13), which fit into grooved slots in the lower jaw when the mouth is closed, and they have a venom that is predominantly neurotoxic (see p.22).

Elapids also lack a loreal scale (on the side of the snout between the nostril and eye), a feature that among colubroids otherwise characterizes only the stiletto snakes (atractaspidine lamprophiids) and a few small colubrids. They occur in all

of the warmer regions of the world except Madagascar, and are particularly well represented in Australia, where they reach their greatest diversity and in terms of different species outnumber all other kinds of snakes.

ABOVE Red spitting cobra, *Naja pallida*, from northeastern Africa. When at rest or on the move, the hood of cobras lies collapsed along the sides of the neck as rather loose skin.

DIVERSIFICATION OF ELAPID SNAKES

Most terrestrial elapids are ground-dwellers, notable exceptions being the arboreal mambas (*Dendroaspis*) and tree cobras (*Pseudohaje*), and the aquatic water cobras (two species of *Naja*), all of which occur in Africa. The family also includes more than 60 marine species, the sea snakes and sea kraits, which, although different in habits and some features of anatomy, are nonetheless closely related and part of the same lineage. Their distinctive appearance is the result of adaptive modifications made necessary for living in the sea, rather than separate ancestry from terrestrial elapids.

Apart from one genus (*Acanthophis*, the death adders) of especially stout, viper-like terrestrial species, elapids are all comparatively slender in build. Many have the appearance of harmless colubrids, and in some this similarity extends also to coloration. The red-yellow-and-black-banded coral snakes of the Americas, for example, bear striking resemblance to various 'mimic' species found in the same areas of distribution (see p.31, p.94). Herpetologists have traditionally recognized several subfamilies of elapid snakes, but do not yet fully understand evolutionary patterns within this large and complex group and so the details of classification within the family are not yet stable. With this in mind, they are grouped here under informal headings that might not always precisely reflect evolutionary relationships.

VENOMOUS OR HARMLESS?

Among the many remarkable features of snakes, one that attracts much interest is the strikingly similar appearance that some harmless types have to certain venomous species. This apparent 'mimicry' appears to have arisen primarily to escape predation, and its survival value is clear. The New World coral snakes, for example, advertise their noxious character with a pattern of red, yellow and black rings that say 'Stop! Danger!', and this livery of aposematic (warning) colours is imitated by no fewer than 115 other species – about 18% of all American snakes. One of the most impressive of all mimics is the harlequin snake, *Pliocercus elapoides*, a dipsadine colubrid from Central America that is known to imitate several different species of elapid coral snake throughout its range and also even their locally specific colour variants (see p.31).

It is not only other snakes that appear to have adopted mimicry as a means of evading predators. Some marine eels are similar in their banded coloration to the venomous

ABOVE LEFT AND ABOVE Spix's coral snake, the elapid *Micrurus spixii* (left) and one of its harmless mimics, the South American colubrine colubrid *Simophis rhinostoma* (right).

sea kraits (the elapid genus *Laticauda*), and a striking mimic of the eyelash palm pit viper, *Bothriechis schlegelii*, from tropical America exists in the unlikely form of a caterpillar. *Hemeroplanes triptolemus* is a species of hawk moth found throughout much of the eyelash viper's range, and the final stage of its larva bears a resemblance to this pit viper. At rest it looks like a twig, but when alarmed it turns its forebody upside down, withdraws its legs into the body cavity, and expands the thorax into a remarkably lifelike impersonation of an eyelash viper's head (see p.88). The whole transformation is completed in just a few seconds. The third and fourth larval stages of *Hemeroplanes* are said to mimic a different snake, the colubrid *Oxybelis aeneus*.

COBRAS, MAMBAS AND OTHER AFRICAN ELAPIDS
Mambas

Among the most feared groups of elapids are the mambas (*Dendroaspis*), which occur only in Africa south of the Sahara. There are five species, of which the black mamba, *D. polylepis*, in particular is infamous for its speed of movement, unpredictable disposition and potent venom. Brownish in colour, it is mostly terrestrial, whereas the other species are predominantly green and live in trees. Mambas (from a Zulu word meaning 'big snake') are large, slender, agile snakes. The black mamba may attain lengths of up to 4.3 m (14 ft) and is extremely fast in its movements: across open ground it has been recorded travelling at speeds of 15 km/h (9 mph), and on downhill slopes is almost certainly capable of moving even faster. The neurotoxic venom of black mambas is fast acting and can be life-threatening within minutes. Just two drops are considered a fatal dose in humans, and with each bite these snakes are capable of injecting up to 20 drops. Like cobras, they are able to flatten the neck, although not nearly to the extent of forming a distinct hood.

The black mamba occurs throughout the eastern half of tropical Africa, favouring dry, open bush country and living in abandoned animal holes, hollow trees or termite mounts. An individual may often take up residence in such a chosen lair for several weeks or even months. They hunt during the day, mostly for bush babies, hyraxes, gerbils and other small mammals, although they have also been observed to eat sugarbirds, snapping them out of the air as the birds hover around flowers, feeding on nectar. In pursuit of prey they may descend underground into rodent burrows and climb high into trees. Black mambas are only 38–61 cm (15–24 in) long when they hatch but grow rapidly: some may reach a length of 1.8 m (6 ft) before they are a year old.

BELOW Black mamba, *Dendroaspis polylepis*. The common name of this elapid snake alludes not to the colour of the body, which is uniform leaden-grey or olive brown, but to the purplish-black lining of the mouth.

Cobras and cobra-like elapids

Cobras and their relatives are distributed throughout much of Africa and Asia. Some grow to considerable lengths. At an adult length of 5 m (16 ft), the hamadryad or king cobra, *Ophiophagus hannah*, is the world's largest venomous snake, while among more than 25 species of 'typical' cobras, *Naja*, the forest cobra, *N. melanoleuca*, may occasionally exceed 3 m (10 ft), and several others reach lengths of 2.5 m (8 ft). A feature for which cobras are especially noted is their ability to spread the skin of their necks into a flattened hood. Several cobras also have fangs specially modified for the purposes of 'squirting' venom (see p.97). Except for the ringhals, *Hemachatus haemachatus*, a viviparous species from Africa, all of them lay eggs, and the females of at least some species also stay with their clutches throughout incubation. Female king cobras, *O. hannah*, take particular care of their eggs by laying them in a nest they build from leaves, often deep inside bamboo thickets, and watching over them until they hatch.

Other African elapids include two species of aquatic cobras, restricted to the vicinity of large lakes. These were previously classified in their own genus (*Boulengerina*), but based on DNA evidence they do not seem to form a lineage entirely separate from 'typical' cobras and so have been transferred to the genus *Naja*. Their bodies are thick and heavy, and the neck can be flattened into a hood, although not to the extent seen in typical cobras. Much of their time is spent diving for fish, their principal food, and they may remain submerged for long periods at a time, but they are also to some extent terrestrial and when not in the water lie in

BELOW A Moroccan specimen of the Egyptian cobra, *Naja haje*.

crevices among rocks near the shoreline or bask in the sun. They grow to a length of about 2.5 m (8 ft). Two species of shield-nosed cobras (*Aspidelaps*) are 50–70 cm (20–28 in) long, stout-bodied snakes that have modified snouts for burrowing through soil and rooting out their prey, mainly frogs and lizards. Both species spread a narrow hood and hiss loudly when alarmed. Also from Africa are two species of tree cobra (*Pseudohaje*), large, slender snakes with very large eyes and long tails, and a small, little-known burrowing species, *Naja multifasciata* (previously classified in its own genus, *Paranaja*). All three are almost hoodless.

Two other genera of cobra-like snakes occur in the Afro-Asian region, and the relationships of these to other Old World elapids is less clear at present. The desert black snake, *Walterinnesia aegyptia*, is a 1 m (3¼ ft) long nocturnal species found in arid habitats of the Middle East, while the other genus (*Elapsoidea*) contains 10 mostly small, burrowing species of garter snakes in various parts of Africa (not to be confused with North American natricine colubrid garter snakes, see p.129).

Previously, cobras, as with several other large and venomous snakes, were considered to comprise relatively few but widespread species. More recent studies including the incorporation of DNA data have resulted in a very different understanding. Nowhere is this more evident than among the 'typical' cobras of the genus *Naja*. In the early 1960s there were only six species recognized, whereas now there are about 26. As well as discovering diversity at the species level, the recent studies have discovered that *Naja* seems to comprise three main lineages (the Asian species, the African spitting species and the African non-spitting species), the latter two groups being each others' closest relative.

DEFENSIVE SPECIALIZATIONS OF COBRAS

LEFT Some snakes are capable of delivering a venomous bite virtually from the moment of birth. Only minutes old, this newly hatched red spitting cobra, *Naja pallida*, is able to defend itself also by squirting venom at an enemy's eyes.

Perhaps no other venomous snakes are more instantly recognizable than the cobras. With its head raised high and neck spread into a flattened 'hood', the appearance of one of these animals primed to defend itself is one of the most impressive spectacles in nature.

All cobras are capable of spreading a hood, which they achieve by extending the specially lengthened ribs of the neck. They normally resort to this behaviour, however, only when threatened. In some species, such as the ringhals, *Hemachatus haemachatus*, and most African species of the genus *Naja*, the hood is marked on the underside with contrasting dark cross-bars, whereas the monocled cobra, *N. kaouthia*, and other Asian species have a single or double eye-like marking on the dorsal surface, which is revealed as the hood is spread.

Several species of cobra also defend themselves by squirting venom. The fangs of these species have an orifice on the anterior surface rather than at the tip, through which venom is forced at high pressure and directed at an enemy in a well-aimed stream, usually at the eyes and face. In certain African species the fangs also have spiral grooves inside that function much like the rifling of a gun barrel, helping to fine-tune the accuracy of the 'spit', as it has become misleadingly known. When 'spitting', the cobra raises its neck well off the ground and tilts its head upwards, holding its jaws widely agape. By curling back the upper lip just enough to expose the orifice of the fang, however, some species can spit with the mouth only partially open, enabling them to perform this feat from almost any position. The effective range to which the venom can be ejected varies between species, but in the larger ones, such as the black-necked spitting cobra, *Naja nigricollis*, it can be as much as 3 m (10 ft). On contact with the eyes the venom causes pain and almost instant temporary blindness, and if left too long before being washed out some permanent loss of sight may result.

Should their hooded threat posture or 'spitting' fail to deter an adversary, some cobra species will, if molested, resort to feigning death, and this extraordinary behaviour can be very convincing. The ringhals, for example, turns over on its side and becomes limp and lifeless with its mouth agape and tongue hanging out and may continue to act in this way even if it is picked up. Most cobras will hiss loudly if threatened, and in the king cobra, *Ophiophagus hannah*, this may take the form of an unusual 'growling' sound.

NEW WORLD CORAL SNAKES

These snakes are best known for their often vivid, red-yellow-and-black-banded colour patterns, which serve as warning signals alerting potential predators to their venomous character. Many animals that eat snakes, particularly birds of prey, appear to have an innate aversion to such markings and instinctively avoid them. There are currently three genera recognized, but there is likely to be taxonomic revision and changes to their classification in the near future. *Leptomicrurus* (with three species), *Micruroides* (one species) and *Micrurus* (more than 70 species) are superficially similar in appearance. The numbers of scale rows around the body and the arrangement of scales on the head are almost constant, and their colour patterns tend also to be similar. Most are confined in distribution to tropical forests, although one species, the harlequin coral snake, *Micrurus fulvius*, occurs in the southern USA, and the Sechura coral snake, *M. tschudii*, and Sonoran coral snake, *Micruroides euryxanthus*, are desert species. They are typically rather slender snakes, with heads scarcely wider than their bodies, short tails and small eyes, and most are strikingly marked with a pattern of red, yellow and black rings. Exceptions include the white-banded coral snake, *Micrurus albicinctus*, from the lowland forests of Brazil, a predominantly black species with contrasting rings of white spots, and the Andean black-backed coral snake, *Leptomicrurus narducci*, characterized by a uniformly dark-coloured body and a red- or yellow-spotted abdomen.

New World coral snakes all have a specialized diet consisting mostly of other snakes, including their own species and other venomous groups such as vipers, but also other elongate and limbless vertebrates such as amphisbaenians and caecilians. Allen's coral snake, *Micrurus alleni*, from southern Central America also eats swamp eels, while the diet of the Surinam coral snake, *M. surinamensis*, seems to be dominated by these and various other fish. Hemprich's coral snake, *M. hemprichii*, from northern South America is particularly unusual in seeming to specialize in eating onycophorans (velvet worms). Coral snakes are all active foragers, and while many appear to be generally nocturnal, others have no particular set pattern of activity.

BELOW The elapid *Micrurus surinamensis* from tropical South America. Despite their potent venom, New World coral snakes often try to hide their heads and draw attention instead to their tails when disturbed. Many less venomous Neotropical snakes have similar colour patterns and possibly mimic coral snakes occurring in the same region. Compare for example *Oxyrhopus rhombifer* (p.131).

The bites of New World coral snakes can be dangerous and perhaps only the small Sonoran coral snake, *Micruroides euryxanthus*, which produces little more than 6 mg ($\frac{1}{5,000}$ oz) of a relatively weak venom, is not potentially lethal to humans. They have rather short fangs and their mouths are relatively small, which has given rise to the myth that these snakes are incapable of biting humans unless they happen to fasten on to a thin piece of skin, such as that between the fingers. Actually, even the smallest species have a surprisingly wide gape and are able to deliver a bite

to almost any part of the body. Although armed with powerful venom and strong warning colours, several species also twitch their whole bodies rapidly in curious, often unnerving, jerking movements that can make it difficult to decide which is the head and which the tail end, providing additional discouragement to potential attackers.

ASIAN CORAL SNAKES AND KRAITS

Asian coral snakes appear to be closely related to the New World forms and, like these species, many have vivid colour patterns. Two species from Southeast Asia are particularly brightly coloured: the blue Malayan long-glanded coral snake, *Calliophis bivirgatus*, and the banded coral snake, *C. intestinalis*, which is brownish with a red or orange dorsal stripe enclosed between two black stripes. The venom glands of these species are especially large, extending under the skin for about one-third the length of the body. In common with most New World coral snakes, they feed on other snakes and are egg-layers. Approximately 11 other coral-snake-like species grouped

A REPRODUCTIVE SUCCESS STORY – THE SHORT-TAILED CORAL SNAKE

RIGHT Short-tailed coral snake, the South American elapid *Micrurus frontalis*, with tail raised in typical defence display.

Coral snakes usually lay their eggs in leaf litter, beneath rotten logs, or in other places similarly conducive to incubation. The short-tailed coral snake, *Micrurus frontalis*, in Uruguay, however, has found a particularly novel way of taking care of its eggs and ensuring that they are provided with optimum conditions. It lays its clutch of one to seven eggs in the nest mound of a particular species of ant, *Acromyrmex lobicornis* – specifically in that part of the nest used by the ants for cultivating a fungus on which they feed. In this underground chamber, the humidity remains more or less constant, and the temperature varies by little more than 2°C (3.6°F), providing an ideal incubation environment for the developing eggs. The ants also clean the eggs, reducing the risk of them becoming contaminated by bacteria or mould, and will even protect them from attack by predatory insects. It is not entirely clear how or indeed if the ants benefit reciprocally from this behaviour, but it may be that the newly hatched coral snakes provide some protection by feeding on amphisbaenians (burrowing, legless, snake-like lizards) and scolecophidian snakes, which are natural predators of ants and often invade their nests.

Other snakes are known to use anthills and also termite nests for incubating their eggs. Among these, the Patagonian green snake (the dipsadine colubrid *Philodryas patagoniensis*) may often lay its eggs in the same ant nests as those used by short-tailed coral snakes.

Malayan long-glanded or blue coral snake, *Calliophis bivirgatus*. This spectacularly coloured elapid occurs throughout much of Southeast Asia. It is nocturnal and secretive.

in the genus *Calliophis* occur over much of Asia, including India and Sri Lanka, southern China, Japan and the Philippines. These are small semi-fossorial species with exceptionally slender bodies and small heads and eyes. They are nocturnal and feed mostly on other reptiles, especially snakes.

Similar to the Asian coral snakes in appearance, although somewhat larger, are the 13 species of kraits (*Bungarus*). Kraits occur over much the same range as Asian coral snakes, and like them also feed chiefly on other snakes. An exception is the many-banded krait, *B. multicinctus*, which eats mainly fish. Most have an enlarged mid-dorsal row of scales and peculiar protrusions on the vertebrae, the precise function of which has not been established but may play some defensive role in body thrashing, to which these snakes often resort when molested. As with coral snakes, some are brightly coloured.

Banded krait, the Asian elapid *Bungarus fasciatus*. This species is among the largest of kraits, with adults reaching lengths over 2 m (6½ ft).

TERRESTRIAL ELAPIDS OF THE AUSTRALO-PAPUAN REGION

The greatest numbers of terrestrial elapid snake species are found in Australia and New Guinea (the Australo-Papuan region), where in places they are the dominant species. In mainland Australia alone there are well over 80 different kinds, compared to some 60 or so of all four other snake families that occur there put together. Almost all are ground-dwelling, and of the few species that occasionally climb, none shows any clear specializations for arboreal life. Quite why there should be so few elapids in the Australo-Papuan region that live in trees, where this habitat is otherwise exploited only by a few pythons and colubrids, is puzzling, but it is interesting that their nearest relatives in Southeast Asia are also mostly ground-dwelling. Perhaps a suitable opportunity for diversification among these forms has never arisen or their ancestors had little natural inclination, need or ability to climb, but this does not seem to be the complete story, especially when it is considered how many other ecological niches in this region are now occupied by elapids.

Australo-Papuan terrestrial elapids do not form a natural group because their last common ancestor also gave rise to the two separate groups of marine elapids, the sea kraits and sea snakes. Thus terrestrial and marine Australo-Papuan elapids together comprise a natural group, the subfamily Hydrophiinae. This is a prolific radiation of venomous snakes that evolved surprisingly rapidly, probably within the last 14 million years or so according to estimates from DNA data.

Taipans, brown snakes and whip snakes

The terrestrial elapids of Australia and the New Guinea region comprise two principal types, one of which includes mostly egg-laying species with a paired row of scales beneath the tail, and the other of which is viviparous with a single row of subcaudal scales. Notable among the larger egg-laying forms, three species of taipans (*Oxyuranus*) are arguably the most fast-moving, unpredictable, and venomous of all Australo-Papuan elapids. Drop-for-drop, the venom of the inland taipan, *O. microlepidotus*, is perhaps more potent than that of any other snake in the world. This species is associated primarily with the flat plains of southwestern Queensland. Related to the taipans are about nine species each of *Pseudechis* and *Pseudonaja*, known variously as 'black snakes' or 'brown snakes' in allusion to their predominant body colour. Among the most widespread, both in Australia and possibly also New Guinea, is the mulga or king brown snake, *Pseudechis australis*, a formidable 2.5 m (8 ft) long species that is often unperturbed in the presence of humans, and reluctant to move away when encountered. A high degree of DNA variation has been found in *P. australis* across its wide range, and it is likely to be classified as several different species eventually. All black and brown snakes are potentially dangerous and, if provoked, some are highly aggressive. A large New Guinea species, the Papuan black snake, *P. papuanus*, is reputed to attack with a tenacity unrivalled by other species, a reputation which has earned it the local name of auguma (meaning 'to bite again'). Brown snakes and black snakes feed on frogs, lizards, small mammals and occasionally birds, and like many elapids in this region, often constrict their prey as well as injecting venom.

ABOVE One of the most formidable of all Australian-Papuan elapids, the taipan *Oxyuranus scutellatus* is also the largest venomous snake in this region. There are authenticated records of examples up to 4 m (13 ft). This example is from Papua New Guinea.

With long slender bodies, more than 10 species of whip snakes (*Demansia*) are among the most agile of all Australo-Papuan elapids. Though normally day-active, they may also be active at night when the weather is warm. Although all are venomous, only large specimens are regarded as potentially dangerous to humans.

Tiger snakes, death adders and other viviparous species

Viviparity is uncommon among terrestrial elapids. In Africa and Asia, only the ringhals, *Hemachatus haemachatus*, and perhaps one or two other species produce offspring by this means, while in tropical America elapids are exclusively oviparous. In Australian elapids, however, viviparity is more prevalent, especially among species found in the cooler, southern part of the continent, and some kinds have relatively large numbers of offspring. The litters of tiger snakes in particular may sometimes contain more than 40, and a female black tiger snake, *Notechis ater*, from Tasmania was observed to give birth to 109 babies, more than has been recorded in any other Australian snake. Tiger snakes are large, up to 2.5 m (8 ft) long, stocky species widely distributed in southern Australia, and black tiger snakes also occur on many of the offshore islands, often in high densities. Males appear to be much stronger than females of the same body size, perhaps because of the strength needed during bouts of ritual male-to-male combat, or because females need to store more fat for reproduction. Also among the largest of Australia's live-bearing elapids are three species of copperhead (*Austrelaps*). Like the tiger snakes, they are more resistant to cold than most other species and can sometimes be found sunbathing even in winter.

A group of about six to ten live-bearing species from Australia, New Guinea and nearby islands that are extremely well camouflaged and have venoms of exceptional potency, are the death adders (*Acanthophis*). Whereas virtually all other elapids are rather slender snakes that actively hunt for their prey, these are sedentary, particularly heavy-set snakes that burrow under leaf litter and lie in wait for small animals to pass within striking distance. As a consequence, they are often difficult to see, and in places represent a serious potential risk – fatal accidents attributed to envenomation by these snakes are reported each year. Their home ranges may be smaller than those of any other elapids, and within an area of only a few square metres they may not move around very much for weeks at a time. Another small adder-like elapid, the bardick, *Brachyaspis curta*, is an exclusively Australian species that feeds mostly on frogs and also uses a 'sit-and-wait' hunting technique.

Three species of broad-headed snakes (*Hoplocephalus*) are slender, nocturnal and the only elapids in Australia that are regularly arboreal. They feed principally on lizards, but occasionally eat frogs and mammals. A jet-black snake dotted with yellow scales, *H. bungaroides* is a particularly spectacular species confined mostly to rocky sandstone habitats from southeastern districts, where its survival is under threat from commercial 'bushrock' collectors. Now classed as endangered, at the time of European settlement during the nineteenth century this snake was common even in the centre of Sydney.

Australian coral snakes, crowned snakes and forest snakes

Several genera of small, mostly egg-laying elapids in Australia and New Guinea are noted for their burrowing habits, defensive displays, and unusual diets. These include 14 species of Australian coral snakes (*Simoselaps*), which are variously marked with red-and-black or yellow-and-black bands and have a specialized diet consisting almost wholly of reptile eggs. Unlike those of other elapids, the teeth on the pterygoid bones in at least one species, the narrow-banded coral snake, *S. fasciatus*, are saw-like. Although sharing the same common name, these Australasian 'coral snakes' are not part of the same lineage as Asian and New World coral snakes. The black-and-white-ringed bandy-bandy, *Vermicella annulata*, is a similarly patterned Australian

ABOVE LEFT Tiger snake, the Australian elapid *Notechis scutatus*.

ABOVE RIGHT Common death adder, *Acanthophis antarcticus*. Death adders are elapids that resemble and behave like vipers. In their native Australia and New Guinea, where there are no vipers, these snakes occupy the same ecological role.

elapid and one of five species in this genus that eat mostly blind snakes (typhlopid scolecophidians). When alarmed, it assumes a curious defensive posture in which the body is elevated in large loops and twisted around, probably as a means of increasing the effectiveness of its black-and-white warning bands. The four species of Australian crowned snakes (*Cacophis*) and perhaps the three species of New Guinea crowned snakes (*Aspidomorphus*) also adopt unusual defensive postures if provoked. The dorsal coloration of these snakes is generally brownish, but the head and neck are more boldly marked with a white or yellowish stripe, and when danger threatens the snakes arch their forebodies off the ground but keep the head pointing directly downwards, thus displaying the colourful head markings to their full effect. Eleven species of forest snakes (*Toxicocalamus*), all of which occur only in New Guinea, are among the very few elapids that feed on invertebrates. Earthworms comprise a large proportion of their diets, but they may also eat insect larvae/pupae and small snails. They are small, secretive snakes and live almost entirely below the surface.

RIGHT Australian banded snake, the elapid *Simoselaps littoralis*.

Small-eyed snakes, Indonesian coral snakes and the Fijiian bola

Although relatively close to Australia in geographical terms, New Guinea, the Solomon Islands and Fiji have a number of elapid snakes that occur only in these areas and are quite distinctive. Most of these are monotypic genera (containing only one species each). During the day, the New Guinea small-eyed snake, *Micropechis ikaheka*, shelters beneath leaf litter and other forest floor debris, or beneath the discarded heaps of coconut husks in plantation areas, where it poses a potential danger to local workers. This essentially banded species has an unusually pale coloration, a feature for which it has become known in parts of its native land as 'white snake'.

Similar to the small-eyed snake is *Loveridgelaps elapoides* from the Solomon Islands, a strikingly marked black-and-white-banded species with patches of bright

ABOVE The small-eyed snake, *Micropechis ikaheka*, is a fairly large – up to 1.5 m (5 ft) long – elapid endemic to New Guinea and adjacent islands, where it is a nocturnal inhabitant of monsoon forests and also occurs in coconut plantations.

yellow on its back. This rarely seen nocturnal elapid occurs mostly near forest streams and feeds on frogs, a habit it shares with another endemic, diurnal species, *Salomonelaps par*. From the island of Bougainville near New Guinea, Hediger's coral snake, *Parapistocalamus hedigeri*, is a small elapid, up to 50 cm (20 in) long, about which very little is known, other than it is a nocturnal, semi-fossorial form that may feed on the eggs of large land snails. Perhaps an even more poorly understood species is the Fijiian ground snake, or bola, *Ogmodon vitianus*. This snake has one of the most isolated distributions of any elapid in the region, occurring only on the small island of Vitu Levu nearly 2,000 km (1,240 miles) from its nearest relatives in the Solomons. Its known distribution appears to be further limited to two adjacent watersheds in the southeastern part of this island. A diminutive burrowing species, only about 20 cm (8 in) long, it is found in forest soils of inland mountain valleys and eats mainly earthworms.

MARINE ELAPIDS – THE SEA SNAKES AND SEA KRAITS

Among the most intriguing of all snakes, in terms of their origins, relationships and specialized life habits, are the sea kraits and sea snakes. The 65 or so species include some of the most completely aquatic of all air-breathing vertebrates, and the only living reptiles that spend all of their lives at sea. With a few exceptions, sea kraits and sea snakes are exclusively marine. Among sea snakes, *Hydrophis semperi* is endemic to a single lake in the Philippine Islands, and *Hydrophis sibauensis* inhabits rivers in Borneo. Among sea kraits, *Laticauda colubrina* and *L. crockeri* inhabit a brackish lagoon (Lake Te-Nggano) on Rennell Island in the Solomons, though the former species also occurs more widely. The two *Laticauda* species in Lake Te-Nggano appear to avoid competition by feeding on different prey, the larger *L. colubrina* on eels and the smaller *L. crockeri* on gobies. Herpetologists once thought that all sea-living snakes (sea kraits and sea snakes) represented a single, divergent line of evolution, but the weight of morphological and DNA evidence now available indicates conclusively that there are at least two principal groups, the sea kraits and the true sea snakes. These are both lineages within the Elapidae, but not each other's closest relative, and they evolved independently from different terrestrial ancestors within the Australo-Papuan region.

The sea kraits (Laticaudini) are the sister lineage to all other Australasian elapids (Oxyuraninae), and this whole group is together termed the Hydrophiinae. Sea kraits drink freshwater, are egg-layers and come ashore to breed. The 'true' sea snakes (Hydrophiini) are deeply nested within the evolutionary tree of Oxyuraninae, and therefore clearly evolved from terrestrial or semi-aquatic Australo-Papuan elapids. True sea snakes are more highly specialized for a marine existence than sea kraits. They are viviparous, and while a few species may occasionally haul themselves out on to rocks or exposed reefs to sun themselves, most never leave the water.

Marine elapids are found in most tropical seas, but are absent from the Caribbean and the Atlantic Ocean. They are essentially creatures of Asian and Australian coastal waters, with only a few species ranging far out to sea. In fact only one species, the yellow-bellied sea snake, *Pelamis platurus*, is truly ocean-going. At times, people have seen large aggregations of certain species floating on the surface of the sea – on one such occasion, in 1932, passengers aboard a steamer passing through the Strait of Malacca off Malaysia reported seeing what must have been a phenomenal number of Stokes' sea snakes, *Astrotia stokesii*, all massed and entwined together in an enormous 'slick', which they said was about 3 m (10 ft) wide and extended for a distance of some 96 km (60 miles)!

Sea kraits

All eight species of sea kraits are included within a single genus, *Laticauda*. As egg-layers, they are more tied to land than the viviparous sea snakes. During the reproductive season they come ashore at night, often in large numbers, on beaches, or in wooded areas at the junction of water and land, with females often depositing their eggs communally in caves. At other times, especially after feeding, sea kraits may also crawl out onto logs floating in the sea or emergent rocks near the tide line to sun themselves. They are good climbers and can sometimes be seen under jetties. Most *Laticauda* are strongly associated with coral reefs and they are familiar to many snorkelers and scuba divers. They have broad ventral scales, legacies of their terrestrial ancestors, blue or yellow colour patterns banded with black, and reach a maximum size of about 2 m (6½ ft). Most feed mainly on eels, which they locate by poking their heads into holes or crevices. As with many aquatic snakes, females are conspicuously larger than males. Females may also feed in shallower water and prey on different kinds of eels than their mates.

In parts of the Philippines, sea kraits used to be very heavily exploited, especially for the leather industry. However, most of these *Laticauda* 'fisheries' have collapsed. The remaining harvest is local and smaller in scale, such as on the islands of Cebu and Luzon, and largely supplies smoked meat to Japan. This same market is also supplied with *Laticauda* collected in the Japanese Ryuku islands.

BELOW Banded or yellow-lipped sea krait, *Laticauda colubrina*, swimming over a coral reef beneath a large shoal of fish, Malaysia.

True sea snakes

Although similar in overall appearance, the Hydrophiini are more specialized for ocean life than the sea kraits. The 16 genera and approximately 60 species are all viviparous and spend their entire lives at sea, although three Australian species at least are more associated with mudflats. In length, they range from as little as 50 cm (20 in) in some species of reef sea snake (*Aipysurus*) to 2.75 m (9 ft) in the yellow sea snake, *Hydrophis spiralis*. The most massively built is Stokes' sea snake, *Astrotia stokesii*, which at an adult length of 2 m (6½ ft) may have a midbody girth of over 25 cm (10 in) and total mass in excess of 2 kg (4 lb 6 oz). Three species of the genera *Ephalophis*, *Hydrelaps* and *Parahydrophis* are restricted mostly to estuaries and mudflats, and seem to retain several relatively primitive features such as broad ventral scales. At the other end of the spectrum, the monotypic yellow-bellied sea snake, *Pelamis platurus*, is a highly adapted, oceanic species with a geographic range greater than that of any other snake or lizard. This species, uniquely marked with a pattern of yellow and black stripes, is found across the Pacific as far west as the western coasts of Central and South America, and as far south as New Zealand and the Cape of Good Hope. It occurs mainly in the narrow strips of calm water where two ocean currents meet, feeding on small fish that congregate around the accumulations of seaweed debris often found floating in these areas.

Adaptive modifications of marine elapids

- The body is flattened from side to side. Stokes' sea snake, *Astrotia stokesii*, a large and unusually stout-bodied species, has a midventral pair of scales enlarged to form a longitudinal keel on its abdomen, which probably acts as a keel-like stabilizer.
- Many species have lost the tight one-to-one association between numbers of vertebrae and numbers of ventral scales, and the broad ventral scales of their terrestrial ancestors have been reduced in width.
- Some species have unusually small heads and narrow necks in relation to their otherwise stout bodies, which enables them to reach deep into holes and crevices to seize gobies and burrowing eels.
- All species have flattened, paddle-like tails with which to propel the body when swimming; in some species, this structure is supported by elongated neural spines (projecting up from the vertebrae) and/or haemapophyses (projecting down from the vertebrae) on the vertebral column of the tail. Olive sea snakes, *Aipysurus laevis*, and perhaps other nocturnal species have photoreceptors (light-sensitive cells) on the tail, which they use to ensure that this end of the body is not left exposed when hiding among crevices during the day.
- The mostly single lung (a very small left lung is retained in a few species) is longer than that of most other snakes (enabling them to stay underwater longer), and stored air can be pumped forward from the saccular part when needed into the vascular part to sustain respiration. The trachea (windpipe) is also developed into a type of lung capable of respiration. Most species are active at depths of less than about 30 m (100 ft), although some might be capable of occasionally diving to 100 m (330 ft) or more. They can stay underwater for at least 30 minutes.

- The nostrils are equipped with valves to keep out seawater. In sea kraits (*Laticauda*) the nostrils are placed on the side of the snout, while in sea snakes they are on the top.
- A modified rostral scale (or in some species an extension of tissue behind this scale) that fits into a notch at the front of the lower jaw seals the opening through which the tongue is normally protruded while the snake is underwater.
- A special salt excretion gland beneath the tongue enables marine elapids to rid themselves of excessive salt. The skin of these snakes is also more impermeable to salt than that of their terrestrial relatives.
- Sea kraits and sea snakes shed their skin more frequently than do terrestrial species, at intervals of 2–6 weeks. This may have some effect in helping to keep the body free of barnacles and other small marine organisms.
- Although their eyes are probably well adapted to the lower intensity and different spectra of light occurring underwater, at least some species are capable of shutting their pupil down to a tiny pinhole when exposed to the much brighter light at the sea surface.

The venom of most marine elapids, although produced only in relatively small amounts, is powerfully neurotoxic (see p.22). Sea krait and sea snake venom is simpler than that of their terrestrial relatives. This streamlining is an adaptation to their fish diet, and it has evolved convergently in a very similar way in these two independent lineages, to such a degree that the same antivenom can work in cases of envenomation from both groups. Sea kraits tend to be docile and may even be handled (not something we recommend) without being bitten, whereas some sea snakes bite readily. The beaked sea snake, *Enhydrina schistosa*, in particular appears to be more aggressive than most and is suspected of being responsible for deaths among Malaysian fishermen.

Fish form the staple diet of most marine elapids, and some species specialize in feeding on particular kinds. Sea kraits (*Laticauda*), for example, hunt for eels among coral

LEFT The hydrophiine elapid *Aipysurus duboisii*, a large species of reef sea snake from the Timor Sea and coastal regions of northern and western Australia.

ABOVE Elegant sea snake, the hydrophiine elapid *Hydrophis elegans*, a species from coastal regions of western New Guinea and northern Australia. Note the paddle-like tail for swimming.

reefs, including potentially dangerous moray eels, which they usually release following the initial strike and leave for the venom to take effect before attempting to consume, while beaked sea snakes, *Enhydrina schistosa*, forage along the muddy bottom of estuaries for catfish. The diet of some species, such as the olive sea snake, *Aipysurus laevis*, also includes crabs and other crustaceans, while others eat only fish eggs. White-spotted sea snakes, *A. eydouxi*, and turtle-headed sea snakes, *Emydocephalus annulatus*, scrape fish eggs off rocks using enlarged anterior labial scales, and it has been suggested that a prominent muscle in the floor of the mouths of these species possibly enables them to also suck out the buried eggs of gobies, blennies and other bottom-dwelling fish. They have a somewhat degenerate venom apparatus and their venom is also relatively weak, an adaptation to a shift away from catching live adult fish.

Sea kraits and sea snakes tend to produce smaller clutches and litters than do their terrestrial relatives. Some species, such as *Praescutata viperina*, produce small litters of three to four relatively large young, whereas others give birth to larger numbers of smaller offspring.

LAMPROPHIIDAE:
The Major Radiation of African Snakes

As explained on p.37, the very large and diverse family Colubridae has recently been reorganized and subdivided, with the creation of several new family-level groups. One of these is the Lamprophiidae, an Old World family with strong representation in Africa, which is closely related (probably the most closely related living group) to the elapids (cobras, mambas, coral snakes and sea snakes). The family Lamprophiidae includes the subfamilies Pseudoxyrhophiinae, Lamprophiinae and Psammophiinae (which are all rear fanged), as well as the burrowing subfamilies Atractaspidinae and Aparallactinae, which are together considered a distinct family in some alternative classifications. There are approximately 300 species of lamprophiids.

SUBFAMILIES ATRACTASPIDINAE AND APARALLACTINAE:
Stiletto Snakes and Centipede-eaters

These two groups of snakes comprise about 65–70 living species. At least some were previously considered by some biologists to be strange vipers, but both morphological and DNA evidence strongly indicates that they are two separate groups that are each other's closest relatives within the family Lamprophiidae, itself more closely related to elapids than to vipers. Aparallactines have fixed, grooved fangs in the rear of the mouth, in which respect they resemble the rear-fanged (opisthoglyphous) 'colubrids', while atractaspidines have hollow, front-mounted fangs superficially like those of vipers. These snakes are mostly adapted for burrowing. Their bodies are cylindrical and of about the same circumference throughout, with no discernible narrowing at the neck. The skull is compact, and the small head often has a projecting snout. Many species have small eyes. The tail is typically very short, and in some species bears a sharp spine at its tip. Some of the larger species grow to just over 1 m (3¼ ft), though most are considerably smaller.

Several atractaspidines and aparallactines are potentially dangerous enough to be considered medically important. The bite of the Natal black snake, *Macrelaps microlepidotus*, in particular, has been known to result in a temporary loss of consciousness, and bites from the larger species of *Atractaspis* may also have serious consequences. The venom is predominantly neurotoxic in its effect (see pp.22, 24), although it also produces local swelling, severe pain and other symptoms more typical of viper bites.

The atractaspidines and aparallactines are essentially African in distribution, with some species ranging into the Near East, and occur in habitats as diverse as rainforest, grasslands and semi-desert. Except for one species, Jackson's centipede-eater, *Aparallactus jacksonii*, they are all viviparous.

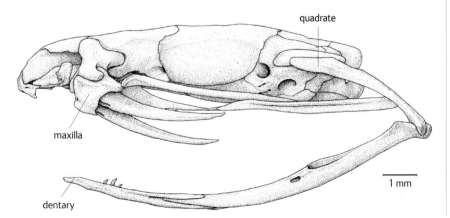

quadrate

maxilla

dentary

1 mm

LEFT Skull of the African stiletto snake, the atractaspidine lamprophiid, *Atractaspis aterrima*. Note the large backward-facing fangs on the upper jaw. On the basis of their dentition, *Atractaspis* species were long believed to be vipers. Unlike vipers, however, the fang-bearing maxillary bone pivots on a lateral ball and socket joint, and the fangs cannot be rotated far forwards.

Subfamily Atractaspidinae: Stiletto snakes

A group of about 19 species, all but one or two atractaspidines are contained within a single genus, *Atractaspis*, with the others in the genus *Homoroselaps*. The stiletto snakes, also known as 'burrowing asps' or 'mole vipers', are remarkable for their disproportionately large, hollow fangs, which are erected independently of each other and extended downwards into a biting position without opening the jaws. There are typically two fangs on each side, one functional and the other a replacement. All other maxillary teeth have been lost, and except for a few on the palatine bones and two or three on the dentaries, the mouth has no other teeth. The venom-injecting apparatus of *Atractaspis* is unusual in a number of other respects, too. Each fang bears a small cutting edge opposite its orifice, and the venom gland in some species, such as the small-scaled stiletto snake, *A. microlepidota*, is extraordinarily long, extending under the skin behind the head for approximately 30% of the body length. The venom itself also has a special composition (see p.24).

Stiletto snakes hunt and feed underground, on rodents and their nestlings but also caecilian amphibians and lizards. Skinks, amphisbaenians (worm-lizards), frogs, and other snakes are also eaten. Without the need to open the mouth to bite, stiletto snakes are capable of killing prey in the most restricted of spaces, including underground burrows. In delivering the predatory strike, a single fang is erected from whichever side of the head is next to the animal, and jerked sideways, downwards and backwards with a quick 'stabbing' movement. The rotating maxilla displaces the upper lip, thus opening a slit through which the fang can be extended. Should a foraging snake encounter more than one rodent at a time, it will typically bite and immobilize all available prey before beginning to feed, and may consume the occupants of an entire nest of mice in this manner if presented with the opportunity.

In response to an assault from a predator, stiletto snakes will arch the neck and strike rapidly with a slashing backwards movement. They bite with little provocation, and owing to their peculiar fang erection mechanism and the unusual flexibility of the neck vertebrae, are very difficult to restrain safely if handled. If molested, an *Atractaspis* may also use the tail-distraction ruse or tail poking (see pp.32, 34).

RIGHT Duerden's stiletto snake the atractaspidine lamprophiid, *Atractaspis duerdeni*, from southern Africa. Stiletto snakes are found throughout much of Africa, with some species ranging into the drier northern part of the continent and also across large areas of Arabia.

Subfamily Aparallactinae: Centipede-eaters and their allies

Aparallactine snakes typically have one or two enlarged, grooved fangs that are situated towards the rear of the mouth and preceded, but not followed, by three to ten smaller, ungrooved teeth. Unlike those of stiletto snakes, the fangs are non-erectile. One species of centipede-eater, (*Aparallactus modestus*) differs in having uniformly sized, ungrooved maxillary teeth. This subfamily includes about 10 genera.

The monotypic Natal black snake, *Macrelaps microlepidotus*, an inhabitant of damp places near water, has the least specialized diet, eating rodents, frogs, legless lizards and a variety of other small vertebrates. Many of the remaining 10 genera, however, have markedly diverse feeding habits.

The 11 species of *Aparallactus* have one of the most unusual dietary habits of any snake. They feed almost exclusively on centipedes, and have enlarged anterior mandibular teeth that perhaps enable them to grasp more effectively the hard, chitinous exoskeletons of these formidable invertebrates. Once bitten, a violent struggle often ensues until the envenomated centipede, which may be over 12 cm (5 in) long and nearly twice the diameter of the snake's body, is sufficiently disabled for the snake to swallow it. The bites of centipedes, which are themselves venomous, appear to have little effect on these snakes. *Aparallactus* occur in rainforest, open bush, sandy regions and savanna, where they are found among roots, beneath stones or fallen logs, and in termite mounds. In general appearance many resemble snakes of the New World colubrid genera *Tantilla* and *Tantillita*, which are also rear-fanged and feed on centipedes.

Nine species of purple-glossed snakes (*Amblyodipsas*) – the common name refers to the purplish sheen of their dark-coloured bodies – are rather stout-bodied snakes in which females appear to grow larger than males. At an adult length of 1 m (3¼ ft), female common purple-glossed snakes, *A. polylepsis*, are almost twice as large as their mates. These species feed largely on reptiles, including limbless lizards, typhlopid snakes and amphisbaenians.

LEFT The aparallactine lamprophiid *Micrelaps vaillanti*, an example from Tanzania.

ABOVE Quill-snouted snake, the aparallactine lamprophiid *Xenocalamus bicolor*, from southern Africa.

A group of five unusual-looking quill-snouted snakes (*Xenocalamus*) derive their name from the resemblance of the prominent snout to that of a quill pen. These species have very slender bodies with flattened heads, minute eyes and acutely pointed snouts with a conspicuously enlarged rostral scale. They occur mostly in sandy regions and feed almost exclusively on amphisbaenians but also some burrowing snakes. Attractively marked with alternating stripes of yellow and black, three species of *Chilorhinophis* are semi-burrowing forms that also live largely on a diet of amphisbaenians. The tails of these snakes are coloured and shaped much like the head, and are used in distracting predators (see p.34).

SUBFAMILY LAMPROPHIINAE:
African House Snakes and File Snakes

Of the 10 genera that are currently assigned to the subfamily Lamprophiinae, some 15 species of African house snakes (*Lamprophis*) are small, 60–90 cm (24–36 in) long, nocturnal constricting snakes that feed mainly on rodents and lizards. With smooth, shiny body scales in numerous rows, fairly short tails and eyes with vertically elliptic pupils, they look rather like hatchling pythons, although they differ in skin pattern. They often visit buildings in search of prey and are useful in controlling vermin. Ten species of African file snakes (*Mehelya*), only distantly related to Asian/Australasian file snakes (*Acrochordus*, see p.72), eat mainly snakes, including venomous species such as night adders and cobras, although they will also consume lizards, toads and

other ectothermic animals. Their common name alludes to the shape of the body, which is triangular in cross-section and resembles a three-cornered file, the abdomen being rather flat and the spine raised into a prominent ridge. The body scales of these snakes are heavily keeled and, unlike those of most colubrids, are contiguous rather than overlapping. In common with other lamprophiines, they are egg-layers.

ABOVE A Tanzanian specimen of the lamprophiine lamprophiid, *Lycophidion ornatum*.

SUBFAMILY PSAMMOPHIINAE:
Sand Snakes, Skaapstekers, Bark Snakes and Beaked Snakes

Another lamprophiid subfamily, the Psammophiinae, includes seven genera of mostly very slender snakes from Africa, Mediterranean Europe and Asia. They have large eyes and prey mostly on lizards and small rodents by sight, often hunting them down at great speed.

More than 30 species of sand snakes (*Psammophis*) and four of skaapstekers (*Psammophylax*) are essentially African in distribution, with one species (*Psammophis condanarus*) in southern Asia and another (*Psammophis lineolatus*) ranging into western China. On a drop-for-drop basis some species have relatively potent venoms, although the quantity expelled is normally too small to cause humans serious illness. Bites from link-marked sand snakes, *Psammophis biseriatus*, and spotted skaapstekers, *Psammophylax rhombeatus*, however, have occasionally resulted in unpleasant envenomation in humans. Other psammophines from Africa include four species of bark snakes (*Hemirhagerrhis*), which are small and rather secretive tree-

ABOVE Olive or hissing sand snake, the psammophiine lamprophiid *Psammophis sibilans*, a large sand snake found throughout much of sub-Saharan Africa in open grassland or bush country.

dwellers, and four species of terrestrial beaked snakes (*Rhamphiophis*), named for their sharply angled snouts.

A large and formidable species that ranges into Mediterranean Europe is the Montpellier snake, *Malpolon monspessulanus*, a 1.8 m (6 ft) long steel-grey snake capable of inflicting venomous bites that have caused clinically significant (but not life-threatening) neurological symptoms in humans. Montpellier snakes and some sand snakes have the habit of smearing themselves with a colourless liquid secreted from glands in the snout, especially after sloughing or feeding. The precise function of this 'rubbing behaviour' is not entirely clear, but because these snakes often live in dry, sun-scorched areas and are sometimes active even during the heat of midday, it may be to help prevent water loss.

SUBFAMILY PSEUDOXYRHOPHIINAE: Madagascan Lamprophiids

The majority of snakes found on the remarkable island of Madagascar are members of the family Lamprophiidae, in particular a group of about 20 genera and over 80 species in the subfamily Pseudoxyrhophiinae. Apart from a couple of species that live on mainland Africa, including the aforementioned snail-eating species from southern Africa (*Duberria*, see p.77) and Günther's racer, *Ditypophis vivax*, which is an endemic of the island of Socotra, the entirety of this subfamily is found on Madagascar and the Comoro Island of Mayotte. Although relatively little is known about the feeding habits of most of these snakes, members of the terrestrial and sometimes burrowing genus *Pseudoxyrhopus* seem to specialize in reptile eggs. The

RIGHT The pseudoxyrhophiine lamprophiid, *Pseudoxyrhopus tritaeniatus* from Madagascar.

stomach contents of a few individuals were found to contain skink and chameleon eggs, all with an intriguing slit down their sides. This may be because reptile eggs are difficult to digest unless the shell is broken, and it has been suggested that the rear fangs of some species may be important for the exploitation of this resource. Feeding on reptile eggs is a relatively well-known practice in burrowing elapids of the genus *Simoselaps*, whose dentition is also highly specialized for this purpose.

COLUBRIDAE: Racers and garter, rat, cat, tree, reed and water snakes and relatives

Until fairly recently, the conception of the family Colubridae was that it contained all 'higher' snakes that were left over after the most distinctive groups (vipers, elapids etc) had been placed in their own families. Snake biologists understood that this was unsatisfactory, but they were somewhat overwhelmed by the morphological and ecological diversity of these more than 1,000 species, and so put up with the situation while continuing their research. More recently, DNA data have been combined usefully with a wealth of existing information on anatomy, and a clearer, more natural classification is beginning to emerge. Additional groups have been demarcated as families (e.g. Homalopsidae, Lamprophiidae) and there is more certainty that those snakes now remaining in the Colubridae represent a single evolutionary lineage. Although we are now able to recognize natural lineages (see p.37), there are still debates as to which groups should be families and which subfamilies, and this might continue to change for some time.

BELOW While most colubrids are egg-layers, the European and western Asian smooth snake, *Coronella austriaca*, is among a small number of species that give birth.

Colubrids are found on all continents except Antarctica and form the main element of snake faunas in many places; only in Australia, where the elapids predominate, and Africa, where lamprophiids are the main radiation, are they clearly in the minority. All species lack a pelvic girdle and coronoid bone (a small bone in the lower jaw primitively retained by some snakes), and many lack a left lung. Some are aglyphous, with unmodified teeth, while others are opisthoglyphous, with enlarged, grooved maxillary fangs towards the back of the upper jaw (see p.13), often connected to a venom-producing gland (Duvernoy's gland) in the mouth. Usually, the venom of these species is lethal only to the animals they feed upon, though there are a few whose bites have occasionally resulted in human deaths (see p.134). In size, colubrids range from diminutive centipede-eating snakes (genera *Tantilla* and *Tantillita*) little longer than a pencil, to the 3.8 m (12½ ft) long Asian keeled rat snake, *Ptyas carinatus*, and, while many are generalist predators that

ABOVE A naturally-occurring colour mutation of the Mexican parrot snake, the colubrine colubrid *Leptophis mexicanus*, from the Turneffe group of islands, Belize. Typical examples of this species are bright green with a bronze-coloured stripe on the back.

feed on a wide variety of different prey, others have special adaptations for highly restricted diets. The latest DNA based study recognizes seven subfamilies within Colubridae (some of which are considered by other workers to deserve family status in their own right), and we follow that classification here. Some of these seven subfamilies are very small, such as the two species in the Scaphiodontophiinae (the Neotropical *Scaphiodontophis annulatus* and *S. venustissimus*), the four species in the Grayiinae (semi-aquatic African snakes in the genus *Grayia*), and the 13 species in the Pseudoxenodontinae (in the East and Southeast Asian genera *Plagiopholis*, *Pseudoxenodon* and *Thermophis*) and are not considered here in any detail. We focus instead on the four major colubrid subfamilies (Colubrinae, Natricinae, Dipsadinae and Calamariinae). This still covers many species of great diversity, so we can sample only a very small number of them in this concise account. In making this selection, however, we feature a broad cross-section of species.

SUBFAMILY COLUBRINAE:
Rat and Tree Snakes, Racers, King Snakes and Allies

More often referred to as typical snakes, rat snakes, racers and king snakes are among a diverse mixture of genera within the subfamily Colubrinae. Some of the common names for these colubrine snakes, especially 'rat snakes' and 'racers', have been applied to various species from different continents that might not be especially closely related, and this can cause confusion. For example, although species of the genus *Coluber* covered here (see below) are known as racers, the same common name is applied often to superficially similar snakes in the Caribbean and South America that are classified in separate genera in a different colubrid subfamily (Dipsadinae, see p.136).

Rat snakes and king snakes

Among the largest colubrines are two species of Asian rat snakes, *Ptyas carinatus* and *P. mucosus*, both of which are reported to exceed lengths of 3.5 m (11½ ft), and there are others that also grow to considerable sizes. The indigo snake, *Drymarchon corais*, in particular, may occasionally exceed 3 m (10 ft) and is almost as robust as some boas and pythons. This widespread New World species occurs in a number of different geographic forms throughout much of Central and South America,

BELOW Tiger rat snake, *Spilotes pullatus*. Although primarily an inhabitant of forests, this large colubrine colubrid species from tropical America also thrives around farms and rural settlements, where it feeds on vermin, and domestic fowl and their eggs.

extending northwards into southern USA. It is a generalist predator that eats a wide variety of vertebrate prey, especially other snakes, and it has a voracious appetite. An almost 3 m (10 ft) long example from Guatemala caught in the act of swallowing a 1.6 m (5¼ ft) long common boa, *Boa constrictor*, already had in its stomach a full-grown jumping pit viper, *Atropoides nummifer*, itself almost 1 m (3¼ ft) in length.

A group of colubrines that constrict their prey and occur mostly in northern temperate regions include eight species of king and milk snakes (*Lampropeltis*) and five species of gopher snakes (*Pituophis*) from the Americas, and various rat snakes (e.g. *Bogertophis*, *Elaphe*, *Senticolis*). Many of these feed on rodents, although their diets typically include a wide range of other prey. King snakes will often eat other snakes, and common king snakes, *L. getulus*, will not hesitate to attack rattlesnakes, copperheads, coral snakes and other highly venomous species.

Racers

Noted for their agility and speed of movement are various genera of slender-bodied colubrines collectively known as 'racers'. About 40 species in the genus *Coluber* include a widespread and often locally abundant species in North America (*C. constrictor*), and others in Europe and Asia. Racers are typically active snakes that hunt by day. Many have conspicuously large eyes and those of eight tropical American species in the genus *Dendrophidion* are especially prominent. They feed chiefly on lizards and frogs, but larger species will also eat small mammals, birds and other snakes. Although primarily ground dwelling, they may be found high above the ground in trees, and some are adept at climbing.

LEFT A Mexican specimen of the coachwhip, the colubrine colubrid *Coluber flagellum*.

BELOW The slender body and large eyes with round pupils of this Central American racer, the colubrine colubrid *Mastigodryas melanolomus*, are characteristic of a fast-moving, diurnal species that hunts down prey by sight, in this case lizards.

RIGHT Asian vine snakes, colubrine colubrids of the genus *Ahaetulla,* have keyhole-shaped pupils, binocular vision, and a long grooved snout that likely assists their view. This species is *A. nasuta* from India and parts of mainland Southeast Asia.

BELOW Green tree snake, *Boiga cyanea*, a rear-fanged arboreal colubrine colubrid from Southeast Asia.

Tree snakes

Among many colubrines that have enlarged fangs in the rear of the mouth and immobilize prey by envenomation, members of three genera in particular are capable of inflicting potentially lethal bites to humans (see p.134). Vine snakes (*Oxybelis* from tropical America, *Ahaetulla* from Asia and *Thelotornis* from Africa) include day-active species that spend almost all their lives in the trees and descend to the ground only rarely. They typically have long, exceptionally slender bodies and narrow, pointed heads with large eyes, and most species have relatively keen eyesight. Other rear-fanged, day-active, tree-living colubrines include five species of Asian flying snakes (*Chrysopelea*), which escape from predators in the treetops by launching themselves off a branch and descending down to the ground or a lower branch in a controlled glide.

Nocturnal rear-fanged colubrines include more than 30 species of Old World tree (sometimes called 'cat') snakes of the genus *Boiga* that have slender bodies, flattened from side to side, and large eyes with vertically elliptic pupils. Essentially tree-dwellers, some grow to impressive sizes. *Boiga cynodon* from Southeast Asia, in particular, may occasionally attain lengths over 2.75 m (9 ft). A strikingly marked black-and-yellow-banded species from Southeast Asia, the mangrove snake, *B. dendrophila*, is relatively stout-bodied and also has a broader diet than most of its relatives, feeding on bats, birds and their eggs, lizards, frogs, other snakes and even fish. Bites from some species of *Boiga* can lead to clinically significant symptoms in humans. Other nocturnal rear-fanged 'cat' snakes include more than a dozen species of *Telescopus*, among which African tiger snakes (*T. beetzii* and *T. semiannulatus*) are strikingly marked yellow-and-black-spotted snakes that feed mostly on geckos and other lizards, but will sometimes climb into trees to rob birds' nests of their eggs and nestlings.

Other colubrines

There are about 70 species of kukri snake in the South and East Asian genus *Oligodon*. These snakes are named after the Nepalese dagger because of their curved rear fangs. They are relatively small, less than 1 m (3¼ ft), mostly nocturnal and oviparous, and many are known to eat eggs. Some *Oligodon* species have brightly coloured undersides and perhaps mimic Asian elapid coral snakes (*Calliophis* species). On Taiwan, *O. formosanus* has been observed preying on green sea turtle nests in such large numbers that fights frequently break out, with many individuals having bitten or even partly missing tails. These *O. formosanus* show true territoriality otherwise unknown for snakes, and females in particular burrow into and try to defend single turtle nests from other snakes so that they can feed on the eggs over several weeks.

Also found in Central and Southeast Asia, as well as Japan, are more than 40 species of wolf-toothed snakes in the genus *Lycodon*. The genus name comes from their distinctive dentition, with three to six fang-like anterior teeth separated by a toothless space from 7 to 15 posterior teeth, the final few of which are much longer than those before them. Many species display bands of darker and lighter pigmentation that are particularly pronounced in juveniles but fade into adulthood. Some, such as the Malayan banded wolf-toothed snake, *L. subcinctus*, closely resemble venomous kraits such as the

A DESTRUCTIVE INVADER – THE BROWN TREE SNAKE ON GUAM

In the 1960s, biologists on the small Pacific island of Guam began to notice that its native bird populations were declining markedly. This trend continued through the 1970s and 1980s until, by 1987, all 10 species of birds that inhabited the island's forests appeared to be in serious trouble. Two found only on Guam and nowhere else, the Guam flycatcher, *Myiagra freycineti*, and the Guam rail, *Gallirallus owstoni*, had not been seen for several years and a previously widespread seabird, the white tern, *Gygis alba*, had become mysteriously restricted to the northern coastline. Native bats and lizards had also declined drastically. A variety of possible causes for this were investigated, including disease, parasites and habitat alteration, but it ultimately became clear that the catastrophe was attributable to a snake, the brown tree snake (the colubrine colubrid *Boiga irregularis*). Indigenous to northeastern Australia, New Guinea and adjacent islands, this 3 m (10 ft) long, rear-fanged venomous species had been accidentally introduced to Guam (a US military base) on cargo shipments shortly after the Second World War, and by 1982 was common almost everywhere on the island, except in a few small areas of savanna.

That a snake could be capable of establishing itself in such numbers as to almost destroy the bird population of an entire island was at first difficult for many to comprehend. Snakes are efficient predators but do not normally occur in large numbers anywhere (although interestingly, the few species that do occur in large numbers generally live on islands and feed exclusively on birds, see p.87). Experiments using traps suspended in trees and baited with quails, however, showed beyond doubt that the brown tree snake was indeed the culprit. In areas where native birds had disappeared, 75% of traps had been sprung and the quails had been devoured within just a few days. It was not only the local wildlife on Guam that suffered. Several young children bitten by brown tree snakes while sleeping had suffered clinical (though not life-threatening) symptoms. By raiding chicken farms and causing many power failures by climbing into transformers and onto overhead cables, the snakes also levied a heavy toll on the island's economy.

In an effort to restore the island in some way to its former natural ecological balance, the numbers of brown tree snakes on Guam are gradually being reduced by trapping. Dogs have been trained to sniff out brown tree snakes in shipping cargo and in the forests. Several zoos are also maintaining populations of the surviving bird species with a view to re-establishing them in the wild. For some of its birds, however, remedial action on Guam has arrived too late.

BELOW Brown tree snake, *Boiga irregularis*.

LEFT The Southeast Asian colubrine colubrid, *Lycodon effraensis*.

Malayan krait, *Bungarus candidus*. Feeding on lizards and frogs, *Lycodon* are oviparous and generally nocturnal and terrestrial, though some are also competent climbers. A large proportion of known species have been discovered in the past decade or so.

Around 18 species of dwarf or peace snakes of the genus *Eirenis* occupy arid and Mediterranean environments from the southeast of Europe throughout the Middle East and parts of northeast Africa. They can often be found on agricultural land and other anthropogenic habitats. They are diurnal or crepuscular and feed primarily on lizards, although soft bodied invertebrates may also form a part of their diet. Occupying a similar, but much larger distribution, are members of the genus *Platyceps*, which can be found as far south as Tanzania and east into northern India and Pakistan. These oviparous snakes are yet another group often referred to as 'racers' and they have a very varied diet consisting of small vertebrates and invertebrates. Although the cliff racer, *P. rhodorachis*, of North Africa and the Middle East is primarily terrestrial, it is an agile climber known to scale trees and thatched roofs in search of eggs. This species will also venture into houses during the day in search of house geckos, birds and mice.

Found throughout the mainland Neotropics, as well as on the islands of Trinidad and St Vincent, 16 or so species of *Chironius* are large (sometimes up to 3 m, 9 ft), active, diurnal snakes known as sipos. Among the best-known members of this genus is the common sipo, *C. carinatus*, with a distribution from Costa Rica to northern Brazil and Peru. Like most of the other species in the same genus, it feeds on anurans and is largely arboreal, spending the nights asleep high up in trees. When disturbed this lowland inhabitant is known to raise its anterior body off the ground, hold its mouth open and hiss. If this does not deter the intruder it will puff up its neck, which it flattens like a hood to expose pale blue skin, and whip its tail back and forth. Male *C. carinatus* also partake in ritual combat during the spring, whereby they intertwine their upper bodies and each tries to get higher than their competitor. This is a behaviour it shares with the two-headed sipo, *C. bicarinatus*, and perhaps other members of the genus.

EGG-EATING SNAKES

ABOVE Egg-eating snake, the colubrine colubrid *Dasypeltis scabra*, from Africa and Arabia.

Various colubrids have highly specialized feeding habits. Conspicuous among these are six species of African egg-eating snakes, *Dasypeltis*, which feed exclusively on birds' eggs and have special structures for dealing with their smooth, hard shells. On the underside of the neck vertebrae are a series of 25–35 bony spines (the hypapophyses) that project downwards like simple teeth. As the snake swallows an egg, it performs a series of sideways and downward rocking movements with its head, during which the egg is forced against these vertebral 'teeth' until ultimately it breaks, often with an audible cracking sound. Muscular contractions of the oesophagus then compress the shell and release its contents into the stomach. The snake expels the crushed empty shell shortly afterwards through its mouth.

So remarkably extensible is the mouth of an egg-eating snake that even comparatively large eggs can be swallowed whole. A 1 m (3¼ ft) long snake with an unextended head scarcely wider than a large fingernail, for example, is quite capable of consuming an average sized chicken's egg. Such incredible feats of swallowing are made possible by a number of modifications that primarily affect the skull. In particular, the supratemporal bones and quadrates (see p.12) are greatly elongated; in most snakes these bones are movably jointed, but in egg-eaters they are fused into an especially movable, free-swinging structure. Furthermore, the lower jaw is long and the ligament that connects each side at the front is highly elastic, enabling the two halves to be stretched widely apart. Inside the mouth itself, there are also loose folds of skin that lie along the lower jaw and unravel during swallowing.

Among various other snakes that eat shelled eggs, the Japanese rat snake, *Elaphe climacophora*, also has spines on the underside of a few anterior vertebrae, but this and all other species swallow the eggs whole and digest everything, including the shell. Only the African egg-eating snakes and maybe a poorly known Indian species, *Elachistodon westermanni* (also a colubrine colubrid), crush and regurgitate the shells.

LEFT Grass snake, *Natrix natrix*, a particularly wide-ranging European natricine colubrid that occurs as far north as 67°N in Scandinavia, and in the southern Alps reaches altitudes up to 2,400 m (7,900 ft).

SUBFAMILY NATRICINAE:
Grass Snakes, Marsh Snakes, Keelbacks, Garter Snakes and Water Snakes

These generally well-known snakes are mostly semi-aquatic and traditionally grouped in the subfamily Natricinae. They are widespread in the Old World and there are also many species in North America, including Canada, Mexico and Central America. Most Old World species lay eggs, whereas the forms from the Americas are viviparous.

From much of Europe, northwest Africa and Asia, four species in the genus *Natrix* are day-active snakes that feed mainly on frogs, newts, tadpoles and small fish. They are usually found in or near water, although some are more aquatic than others. The dice snake, *N. tessellata*, in particular, spends much of its time in water and often remains beneath the surface for considerable periods, while others may often be encountered in dry heathlands, meadows and woods. European *Natrix* are mostly green snakes marked with variable patterns of spots or indistinct stripes, although the viperine snake, *N. maura*, often has a zigzag pattern that increases its resemblance to a viper. By hissing fiercely, flattening its body and striking repeatedly (though usually with its mouth closed) when cornered, the behaviour of this species is also convincingly viper-like.

African natricines (marsh snakes)
Natricines from tropical Africa include several species of marsh snakes, *Natriciteres*, and various other water-dwelling species (of the genera *Afronatrix* and *Hydraethiops*) that feed chiefly on frogs. Some also eat fish and aquatic invertebrates. Marsh snakes are unusual among snakes in being able to break off their tails to escape from predators, although unlike that of many lizards, the tail does not grow back once broken. Among the most widespread, the African olive marsh snake, *N. olivacea*, ranges from Ghana and Sudan to Angola, Zimbabwe and southern Mozambique, in streams and marshes from sea level up to about 1,980 m (6,500 ft).

RIGHT Garter snakes are found in a wide range of different habitats but usually near pools and other bodies of freshwater. Among the more thoroughly aquatic is the twin-striped garter snake, the natricine colubrid *Thamnophis hammondii*, from southern California and Mexico.

Asian natricines (keelbacks)

Asian natricines include various genera, collectively called 'keelbacks', that live in a wide range of habitats and feed mainly on amphibians and fish. Among the most widespread, the approximately 10 species of *Xenochrophis* are largely aquatic and commonly referred to as painted keelbacks. The chequered keelback, *X. piscator*, is a particularly common species found throughout much of southern Asia where it occurs in weed-choked ponds, slow-flowing rivers, streams, ditches and flooded rice paddies. A group of nearly 20 species found mostly in highland areas, the stream snakes (the genus *Opisthotropis*) eat mostly earthworms, while the bicoloured stream snake, *O. lateralis*, resembles some North American natracines, (crayfish snakes of the genus *Regina*) in its striped body markings and diet of crustaceans. Notable among Asian keelbacks for their potentially dangerous bites are almost 20 species in the genus *Rhabdophis*. Most are generally mild-mannered and docile, but they have much-enlarged rear fangs and the venom of at least two species is unusually potent (see p.134). Many Asian natricines flatten their necks when alarmed, and *Macropisthodon* and some species of *Rhabdophis* discharge a distasteful whitish secretion at the same time from glands in the neck. The East Asian yamakgashi, *R. tigrinus*, can make this gland secretion poisonous by sequestering poisons from toads that it eats, with the amount of poison held in the glands depending on the amount of toads in the diet.

American natricines (garter snakes and 'water' snakes)

This final group of natricines is found in the New World. Commonly referred to as water and garter snakes they represent a single evolutionarily lineage that probably originally dispersed to the Americas from the Old World. These natricines are not to be confused with African 'garter snakes' (species of the elapid genus *Elapsoidea* (see p.96). Among the most widespread and common of these are some 30 species of garter and ribbon snakes, *Thamnophis*, that are largely found in the USA, although several range into southern Canada and some also live in Mexico and northern Central America. Often brightly coloured, with contrasting patterns of dorsal stripes and spots, they are small- to medium-sized, rather slender snakes with strongly keeled scales. Northwestern garter snakes, *T. ordinoides*, and western terrestrial garter snakes, *T. elegans*, in particular, are often found far from water, while others, such as western aquatic garter snakes, *T. couchii*, and narrow-headed garter snakes, *T. rufipunctatus*, are highly aquatic. Garter and ribbon snakes feed chiefly on amphibians, small fish, earthworms and aquatic invertebrates such as leeches. The common garter snake, *T. sirtalis*, sometimes preys upon the rough-skinned newt, which carries a potent neurotoxin in its skin, and it has been shown that the snakes retain the newt toxin in their livers for up to several weeks, in quantities that probably makes them poisonous to bird or mammal predators.

Widely distributed over large parts of eastern and southern North America, there are about 10 species of highly aquatic snakes in the genus *Nerodia*. Although they are commonly referred to as water snakes, this is a name they share with many other genera across several families and geographical regions and so can be confusing.

ABOVE Green water snake, the natricine colubrid, *Nerodia cyclopion*, largest of the North American water snakes and one of the most fecund snakes in this region. Adult females may produce more than 100 young in a single litter.

These are stout-bodied forms with strongly keeled dorsal scales and sombre-coloured markings. Females often grow considerably larger than males and those of some species, such as the green water snakes (*N. cyclopion* and *N. floridana*) and the brown water snake, *N. taxispilota*, may occasionally grow to over 1.5 m (5 ft). Water snakes are almost always found near ponds, streams, bayous, canals and lakes, particularly where there is dense aquatic vegetation and little current, although Harter's water snake, *N. harteri*, of Texas is restricted mostly to clear, swift-flowing streams and rivers, and salt-marsh snakes, *N. clarkii*, occur mostly in brackish estuaries.

Other water-living natricines from North America include the black swamp snake, *Seminatrix pygaea*, and four species of crayfish snakes (*Regina*). These thoroughly aquatic species are typically found coiled among the matted roots of water hyacinth and other floating vegetation, where they feed on frogs, small fish, shrimp, crayfish and other aquatic invertebrates. Crayfish, in particular, feature heavily in the diets of several species, and the queen snake, *Regina septemvittata*, appears to feed almost exclusively on newly moulted crayfish whose shells have not yet hardened.

The four species of brown-and-red-bellied snakes, *Storeria*, three of earth snakes, *Virginia*, and Kirtland's snake, *Clonophis kirtlandi*, are among a number of other North American and Mexican natricines that, although often found near water, are entirely terrestrial. These species mostly eat invertebrates and live among leaf litter in wooded areas or grass in wet meadows.

SUBFAMILY DIPSADINAE: New World Snail-eating Snakes, Cat Snakes, Mussuranas, False pit Vipers and Allies

This ecologically and morphologically diverse group of snakes has undergone several changes in its classification. Some classifications have afforded this group full family status (variably called Dipsadidae or Xenodontidae) and considered it to contain two or three subfamilies, but here we treat it as a single subfamily of the Colubridae. Dipsadinae numbers more than 700 species, making it the most prevalent major group of snakes in the New World (to which they are restricted). Dipsadines are mostly tropical, occurring in South and Central America and the Caribbean, but a few species extend also into North America. There are two main branches in the evolutionary tree of Dispadinae – those species more closely related to *Dipsas*, and those more closely related to *Xenodon*. The North America dipsadines might comprise a third major branch but this is not yet clearly resolved.

LEFT *Oxyrhopus rhombifer*, a rear-fanged but only mildly venomous dipsadine colubrid from tropical South America. Compare with *Micrurus surinamensis* (p.98), a more venomous elapid found in the same region.

New World snail-eating snakes, cat snakes and blunt-headed snakes: *Dipsas* and relatives

As mentioned earlier (see p.76), several dipsadine genera (*Dipsas*, *Sibon*, *Sibynomorphus* and *Tropidodipsas*) share a specialization with members of the Southeast Asian family Pareatidae in that they feed almost entirely on snails and slugs. Although not closely related, both dipsadine and pareatid snail-eaters use a similar technique to remove the soft bodies of their gastropod prey, and all of these snakes are similarly small with large heads and protruding eyes. The ringed snail-eater, *Tropidodipsas sartorii*, from Central America has a cylindrical body and is a ground-dwelling inhabitant of forest leaf litter, whereas the cloudy snail-eater, *Sibon nebulata*, short-faced snail-eater, *Dipsas brevifacies*, and most others are adapted for climbing, with long bodies flattened from side to side, and the head strongly differentiated from the slender neck.

Among other species usually grouped in the Dipsadinae are six species of blunt-headed snakes (*Imantodes*). They are nocturnal and feed chiefly on small *Anolis* lizards, often plucking them from leaves and branches as they sleep. Closely related, but more robustly built, are 10 species of cat-eyed snakes (*Leptodeira*). These feed on a wide range of prey, including other snakes, although they are generally considered to be mostly frog-eaters. The small-spotted cat-eyed snake, *L. septentrionalis*, eats the egg masses of leaf-breeding tree frogs, to which they may be attracted by the vibrations generated by the loud calls of breeding frogs.

Several snakes on the *Dipsas* branch of the dipsadine evolutionary tree, including *Adelphicos*, *Geophis* and *Atractus*, live mostly underground, chiefly on a diet of earthworms. With over 130 species described and new ones frequently being discovered, the genus *Atractus* has more species than any other snake genus, and more than almost any other amniote (the group including reptiles, birds and mammals). *Atractus* range from

BELOW The dipsadine colubrid, *Leptodeira septentrionalis*, sometimes feeds on egg masses of tree frogs, such as these of the red-eyed tree frog, *Agalychnis callidryas*, in Costa Rica.

southern Central America to the south of Brazil, and from the Pacific slopes of the Andes to the Atlantic rainforest of South America. Many species appear to have very restricted geographical ranges, particularly those found in the Andes. However, many species of *Atractus* are known from only one or very few specimens, and as with many small burrowing snakes much remains to be discovered about their biology. Commonly known as ground snakes, they are generally small (around 20 cm, 8 in), although the giant ground snake, *Atractus gigas*, is much larger than the rest and can reach over 1 m (3¼ ft) long.

ABOVE Yellow blunt-headed snake, the Neotropical dipsadine colubrid, *Imantodes inornatus*. The slender, laterally compressed body, long tail, and large eyes with vertically-elliptic pupils are characteristic of snakes that live in trees and hunt by night.

LEFT The dipsadine colubrid, *Atractus tamessari*, from Guyana is one of more than 130 species in this genus.

POTENTIALLY DANGEROUS COLUBRIDS

ABOVE Boomslang, the colubrine colubrid *Dispholidus typus*, in characteristic defence posture. Boomslangs are widely distributed throughout much of Africa, and are entirely arboreal in habits. They feed mainly on small birds and lizards, especially chameleons.

Many colubrids have enlarged (but not hollow) fangs in the rear of the mouth and approximately one-third of all colubrids produce venom in mouth glands (called Duvernoy's glands) that are somewhat dissimilar to the venom glands of vipers and elapids. Until just over 50 years ago it was believed that all colubrid bites were generally harmless to humans. The death in 1957, however, of a prominent herpetologist following the bite of a boomslang (the African colubrine *Dispholidus typus*), set alarm bells ringing that changed this view rapidly.

People who have experienced the effects of boomslang envenomation as well as the venoms of other potentially dangerous African species such as cobras have remarked that, by comparison, the bite of the boomslang is by far the most painful and distressing. Among the worst of its unpleasant symptoms is profuse internal bleeding. The boomslang is generally an inoffensive snake that tends not to bite unless it is seriously provoked, but its venom is evidently potent. Remarking on which of Africa's snakes he considered the most venomous, Richard M Isemonger, a distinguished African herpetologist and author of several books on snakes, placed the boomslang right at the top, above even the infamous mambas (the elapid *Dendroaspis*).

Bites from various other rear-fanged colubrids have also been known to cause clinically significant symptoms in humans. In particular, those of African vine/twig snakes (the colubrine colubrid *Thelotornis*) have caused several fatalities, including the death in 1972 of an eminent German herpetologist, Robert Mertens, and more recently deaths have been recorded following bites inflicted by an Asian species of keelback (subfamily Natricinae), the yamakagashi, *Rhabdophis tigrinus*. Other colubrids that appear to have particularly potent venoms include Asian cat/tree snakes (the colubrine genus *Boiga*) and among the subfamily Dipsadinae, the Central American road guarder, *Conophis lineatus*, and some Neotropical racers, particularly those of the genus *Philodryas*.

Despite these cases, most colubrids are not venomous. Even the venomous species by and large pose no special health risk to humans in the wild because envenomation is exceptionally rare and occurs almost invariably during direct handling.

Mussuranas, false pit vipers and Neotropical water snakes: *Xenodon* and relatives

The *Xenodon* branch of the dipsadine evolutionary tree comprises a diverse group of mostly South American snakes. They include more than 10 species of mussuranas (in the closely related genera *Clelia* and *Mussurana*), renowned for their capacity to overpower and eat venomous pit vipers. Some mussuranas undergo a striking colour change with age. Juveniles are bright orange-red with a black head and pale neck ring, but when they reach about 60 cm (24 in) in length they gradually darken, and with successive moults of the skin eventually change to a uniform deep bluish-black.

Five species of false pit vipers (*Waglerophis* and *Xenodon*) have colour patterns strikingly similar to those of some pit vipers; when provoked, these frog and toad-eating snakes recoil and hiss loudly, as many pit vipers do, and also flatten their necks. Over a dozen species of Neotropical water snakes (*Helicops*) display several classic adaptations to aquatic life, including eyes and nostrils on the top of the head and viviparity. One member, *Helicops leopardinus*, is an abundant species in the giant Pantanal wetland region of Brazil. Like its congeners this species feeds largely on

BELOW False pit viper, the dipsadine colubrid *Waglerophis merremi*, from South America. The enlarged fangs of this opisthoglyphous species can be seen in the rear of its mouth. Note also the extensive mouth cavity and forward-placed opening of the windpipe, modifications that enable snakes to swallow large prey.

fish, with frogs making up a lesser but considerable part of the diet, and it actively forages in both shallow pools and at the bottom of deeper water. It is often found in association with floating vegetation, a microhabitat that supports large numbers of small fish. The genus *Liophis* includes many species also commonly found in wet lowland areas.

Other South American dipsadines on the *Xenodon* branch of the evolutionary tree include three species of false water cobras, *Hydrodynastes*, and almost 20 fast-moving snakes in the genus *Philodryas*. A semi-arboreal species from Brazil (*Tropidodryas striaticeps*) is unusual among colubrids in having a long, thin prehensile tail. Juveniles of this species have a yellow-white tail with flared scales and they have been observed undulating the tip as a lure to attract lizards and other prey items. This species also actively forages, and larger prey items such as rodents are often constricted, particularly by adults, although they are probably also subdued with the use of venom.

One lineage of dipsadine snakes dispersed from the South American mainland and into the Caribbean, where it diversified over the last 10 million years (based on DNA evidence) into more than 40 species (in 10 genera). These West Indian 'racers' are now classified in their own tribe, Alsophiini. Most West Indian racers are ground-dwelling and generally brownish, like their probable South American ancestor, but three species of the genus *Uromacer* on the island of Hispaniola are green and arboreal. The West Indian racers were previously thought to be closely related to superficially similar snakes of the Galápagos islands, but information on hemipenis morphology now suggests that this is unlikely, and further DNA analysis is expected to confirm that the Galápagos species are a separate radiation.

RIGHT Mussurana, *Clelia clelia*, a powerful 2.5 m (8 ft) long Neotropical species that frequently predates on venomous snakes and is largely immune to the highly toxic venom of pit vipers.

SUBFAMILY CALAMARIINAE: Asian Reed Snakes

Nine genera and about 80 species of reed snakes grouped in the subfamily Calamariinae are small – up to about 45 cm (1½ ft) long – shiny-scaled snakes found mainly in Southeast Asia. They are adapted for burrowing, with slender, cylindrical bodies, fused head scales and a rigidly constructed skull. If disturbed on the surface, they often wriggle down into the soil at speed. In both skin patterns and behaviour some are superficially but strikingly similar to some highly venomous elapids. Pink-headed reed snakes, *Calamaria schlegeli*, for example, are deep bluish-black with a bright orange-red head, like both the Malayan long-glanded coral snake, *Calliophis bivirgatus*, and the red-headed krait, *Bungarus flaviceps*. All calamariines are oviparous and they eat mostly earthworms and insect larvae, although the diet of some larger species, such as *Calamaria lumbricoidea*, also includes skinks. The dwarf reed snake, *Pseudorabdion longiceps*, is a relatively common species from Indonesia, Malaysia and Thailand. Usually less than 20 cm (8 in) long, it inhabits low-lying forests and cultivated areas such as rice paddies. Like most calamariines it is semi-fossorial and is most often encountered when looking under stones and in damp decaying plant matter. This subfamily is intriguing because so little is known about the natural history of any of its members. With 10 new species of Calamariinae having been described in the last five or so years, there is much still to learn about this group.

LEFT The calamariine colubrid, *Calamaria grabowskyi*, from Borneo.

Glossary

ADAPTIVE RADIATION the evolution of a natural group (see p.37) of species into a diverse range of forms adapted for different niches

AESTIVATION extended dormancy during periods of heat and/or drought

AGLYPHOUS simple dentition; lacking fangs (see p.13)

AMNIOTE a member of the Amniota – the group of vertebrate animals with multiple membranes surrounding the embryo within the egg, including living reptiles, birds and mammals

ANTIVENOM biological product for treating venomous bites, made by collecting antibodies produced when dilute venom is injected into domestic mammals

ANURANS members of the amphibian order Anura – frogs and toads

APOSEMATIC colour and patterning that serves to warn off predators, often advertising the dangerous nature of an animal

AQUATIC living in water

ARBOREAL living in trees

ASPHYXIATE to restrict oxygen, for example by suffocation

AUTOHAEMORRHAGE spontaneous bleeding behaviour that has evolved in some snakes (e.g. genus *Tropidophis*) probably as a means of deterring predators

AUTOTOMY shedding part of the body, usually the tail, either spontaneously or when grasped by a predator

BRILLE transparent covering to eye in most snakes, also called the spectacle

CARNIVOROUS meat-eating

CARRION dead meat eaten by scavengers

CHEMORECEPTION odour detection; the senses of taste and smell

CHYME partly digested food passed from the stomach to the intestine

CLOACA the common chamber into which the reproductive and digestive tracts discharge their contents, emptying to the outside through the vent

CONGENER a species classified within the same genus

CONSTRICTION method of disabling or killing prey by coiling tightly to restrict breathing and blood flow

CONVERGENT EVOLUTION the independent acquisition of similar features by species that are not especially closely related, often in response to a similar way of life

CORONOID a small bone of the lower jaw found in some snakes that retain this primitive feature (see p.12)

CREPUSCULAR active at dawn and dusk, during twilight

DENTARY the front, main tooth-bearing part of a snake's lower jaw (see p.12)

DIURNAL active during the day

DORSALS scales on the body of a snake except those along the midline of the belly (ventrals)

DUVERNOY'S GLAND venom-producing gland in the mouth of rear-fanged colubrid snakes, named after D.M. Duvernoy, a French anatomist. Duvernoy's glands are somewhat dissimilar to the venom glands of vipers, elapids and atractaspidine lamprophiids, but they might nonetheless have evolved from the same ancestral structure

ECTOPTERYGOID a bone in the upper jaw forming part of the roof of the mouth (see p.12)

ECTOTHERMIC dependent on external (environmental) conditions to regulate body temperature

FOSSORIAL burrowing

GASTROINTESTINAL of the stomach and intestine

GASTROPOD a snail or slug, a member of the mollusc class Gastropoda

GLOTTIS entry to the tube (the trachea) that leads to the lungs

HAEMAPOPHYSIS small bone projecting downwards from the underside of a tail vertebra

HAEMOTOXIC action of a toxin that primarily attacks the blood and circulatory system

HEMIPENIS (PL. HEMIPENES) one of the paired male copulatory organs of snakes (see p.10, p.26)

HERPETOLOGY the study of amphibians and reptiles

HIBERNATION extended dormancy during cold periods

HYPAPOPHYSIS ventral projection on a vertebra in the body of a snake

HYPOTENSIVE SHOCK sudden low blood pressure

HYPOVENTILATE inadequate ventilation of the lungs caused by slow or shallow breathing

INFRARED electromagnetic radiation that has a wavelength longer than visible light

INTERNASALS a typically paired set of scales on the top of a snake's snout approximately between its nostrils

JACOBSON'S ORGAN see vomeronasal organ

KEELED having a keel or ridge

KERATIN a group of proteins that are the main toughening components of scales, also found in claws, hair and skin

LABIALS head scales along edges of a snake's upper and lower lips

LOREAL a scale on the side of a snake's snout between the nostril and eye, but touching neither

MANDIBULAR of the lower jaw (the mandible)

MARINE living in sea water

MAXILLA a bone in a snake's upper jaw (see p.12)

MELANOPHORES pigment-containing cells in the skin

MENTAL GROOVE midline cleft between the scales on the underside of the chin in some snakes

METABOLIC RATE amount of energy expended by an animal when at rest

MICROORNAMENTATION microscopic surface features, such as on scales

MICROVILLI microscopic projections on the surface of some cells that facilitate absorption and secretion

MIMICRY resemblance of one species to another, often distasteful or harmful species

MONOTYPIC lineage (e.g. genus or family) represented by only a single known species

MORPHOLOGY form, structure and appearance – or the study of those aspects of organisms

MYOTOXIC activity of toxins that destroy muscle tissue

NEURAL SPINE the dorsal projection on a vertebra

NEUROTOXIC activity of toxins that have a particularly marked effect primarily on nerve tissues

NEW WORLD the Americas

NICHE ecological role/position

NOCTURNAL active during the night

OESOPHAGOUS the muscular tube between the mouth and stomach

OLD WORLD the continents of the eastern hemisphere known before the discovery of the Americas, i.e. Europe, Asia, and Africa

OLFACTORY relating to the sense of smell

OPISTHOGLYPHOUS having fangs toward the back of the mouth; rear-fanged (see p.13)

OVIPAROUS egg-laying

PALATINE a bone of the palate (roof of the mouth) that bears teeth in many snakes (see p.12)

PARASITIC lifestyle whereby one organism (parasite) benefits at the expense of another (host)

PELVIC GIRDLE the hip (pelvis), connecting the hindlimb to the body

PHEROMONES biochemical produced by one organism that triggers a response in another of the same species; for example, sex pheromones convey information about species identity and reproductive condition

PHOTORECEPTION: process by which the eye detects light

PHYSIOLOGY the function of living organisms, also the study of this

PREHENSILE able to grasp

PREMAXILLA a small bone on the front end of the snout that in some snakes bears small teeth (see p.12)

PROCRYPSIS colour and patterning designed to conceal an animal in its natural habitat

PROTEROGLYPHOUS having fangs in the front of the mouth that are largely immovable (see p.13)

PTERYGOID an often tooth-bearing bone in the back of the roof of the mouth (see p.12)

QUADRATE a bone in the back of the skull that articulates with the lower jaw

RECTILINEAR type of locomotion in which a snake moves slowly forwards in a straight line, without bending the body

RETINA light-sensitive lining of the inner surface of the eye

ROSTRAL SCALE the scale at the tip of a snake's snout

SEXUAL DIMORPHISM male/female differences in morphology

SIDEWINDING type of locomotion in which only small areas of a snake's body are in contact with the ground at any one time and in which the body does not move while in contact with the ground, particularly used by vipers to move on loose sand

SOLENOGLYPHOUS having fangs in the front of the mouth that are hinged and erectile (see p.13)

SPECIES COMPLEX group of closely related, usually similar-looking species in which the exact boundaries between (or exact number of) species are unclear

SQUAMATES reptiles of the order Squamata, comprising lizards and snakes

STAPES a small bony rod at the back of the skull through which sound vibrations are transmitted to the inner ear (see p.12, p.18)

STERNUM the breastbone – absent in snakes

SUBCAUDALS the scales on the underside of the tail

SUPRATEMPORAL a bone that links the quadrate and lower jaw assembly with the back of the skull (see p.12)

TERRESTRIAL living on land

THORAX chest and upper body

TOXIN poisonous substance

TRACHEAL LUNG an additional respiratory organ attached to the windpipe

TRANSVERSE crossing from side to side, at right angles to the long axis

TYPE LOCALITY locality from which the specimen used to first describe a new species was collected

VENOM substance containing toxins that is injected into prey (or attackers) by biting

VENTRALS scales along the midline of the underside of a snake's body

VIVIPAROUS giving birth to young rather than laying eggs, commonly termed 'live-bearing'

VOMERONASAL ORGAN organ in the roof of the mouth for sensing odour, especially those chemicals picked up by tongue-flicking

Further information

FURTHER READING

Australian snakes: a natural history, Richard Shine. Reed Books, Sydney, 1991.

Boas and pythons of the world, Mark O'Shea. Princeton University Press, 2007.

The dangerous snakes of Africa, Stephen Spawls and Bill Branch. Blandford Press, London, 1995.

The new encyclopedia of snakes, Chris Mattison. Princeton University Press, 2007.

Homalopsid snakes: evolution in the mud, John C. Murphy. Krieger Publishing Company, 2007.

Mean and lowly things, Kate Jackson. Harvard University Press, 2008.

Sea snakes, 2nd edn., Harold F. Heatwole. Krieger and University of New South Wales, 1999.

Secrets of the snake charmer, John C. Murphy. iUniverse, Bloomington, 2010.

Snakes: a natural history, Roland Bauchot. Sterling, New York, 2006.

Snakes: Smithsonian answer book, George R. Zug and Carl H. Ernst. Smithsonian Institution Press, Washington, 2004.

Snakes: the evolution of mystery in nature, Harry W. Greene. University of California Press, Berkeley, 1997.

Tales of giant snakes: a historical natural history of anacondas and pythons, John C. Murphy and Robert W. Henderson. Krieger, 1997.

Venomous snakes of the world, Mark O'Shea. Princeton University Press, 2011.

INTERNET RESOURCES

The Reptile Database: www.reptile-database.org

[comprehensive listing of all living reptile species with details of distribution and classification]

Index

Acknowledgements

PICTURE CREDITS

Cover © Michael D.Kern/naturepl.com; p.6, 39, 53 left, 113, 115 © 2012 by michelemenegon.it; p.7, 17 left, 21, 24, 30, 31, 35, 51, 56, 58, 59, 63, 67 below, 82, 86 right, 88, 93, 95, 97 left, 117, 118, 119, 120 right, 121, 127 © Peter Stafford/NHMPL; p.8 © Jean-Claude Rage; p.9 Kenney Krysko/University of Florida; p.10 top right © Colin Keates/Dorling Kindersely/gettyimages; p.10 right, 112, 114, 136 © Minden Pictures/Superstock; p.11, 12, 13, 43, 44 right, 46 right, 111 Brian Groombridge; p.15, 19, 20, 40, 45, 52, 61 left, 64, 65 left, 71, 77, 100 top, 120, 121 below right, 126, 128, 130 © Chris Mattison; p.17 above, 23, 25, 34, 46 below, 81, 83 above, 86 above, 87, 89 below, 94, 96, 99, 122, 131, 133 above, 135 © Wolfgang Wüster; p.27 © Tony Phelps/naturepl.com; p.28 © Tim Allen; p.33 below left © Jean Paul Ferrero/ardea.com; p.33 left, 42 above, 47 left, 49, 50, 53 below, 61 below left, 74, 80 right, 83 left, 84 right, 85, 90, 97 top, 100 bottom, 102, 103, 116 above © Stephen von Peltz; p.38 © George Zug; p.42 below, 133 left © Philippe Kok, Royal Belgian Institute of Natural Sciences; p.44 above, 55, 104, 109, 110 © Steve Swanson; p.47 above, 137 Photo: Indraneil Das; p.48, 66 below right © Ashok Captain; p.60, 67 above, 105, 124 © Mark O'Shea; p.65 © Jonathan Campbell; p.66 right © Benny Trapp/Wikimedia Commons; p.68 © Richard Gibson; p.69 © Wolfgang Grossman; p.73, 76 © David Gower; p.78 © Thomas Eimermacher; p.80 below, 134 © Steve Spawls; p.84 below right © Behzad Fathinia; p.89 above © NHMPL; p.91 © John C.Murphy, JCM Natural History Photography; p.98 © NHPA/Daniel Heuclin; p.107 © David Fleetham/bluegreenpictures.com; p.116 right © M.Vences; p.125 © Gernot Vogel; p.132 © Katie Garrett.

NHMPL, Natural History Museum Picture Library

Unless otherwise stated, images are copyright of the Natural History Musem, London

Every effort has been made to contact and accurately credit all copyright holders. If we have been unsuccessful. We apologise and welcome correction for future editions.

AUTHOR'S ACKNOWLEDGEMENTS

David Gower and Katherine Garrett thank the following people for expert reviews, advice, information and encouragement while writing this new edition: Trudy Brannan, Karin Fancett, S. Blair Hedges, Barry Hughes, Kate Jackson, Simon T. Maddock, Anita Malhotra, Colin J. McCarthy, John C. Murphy, Kate L. Sanders, Wulf D. Schleip, Alessandra Serri, Gemma Simmons and Mark Wilkinson. We thank the skilled fieldworkers, artists and photographers who provided images for use in this book, and also acknowledge the people thanked by Peter Stafford in the previous edition.